BALLATTIS OF LUVE
1400 – 1570
*

Adew, fair Snawdoun, with thy touris hie,
thy Chapell Royall, Park and Tabyll Rounde.
Lindsay *Testament of the Papyngo*, 633–4

BALLATTIS
OF LUVE

EDITED, WITH
AN INTRODUCTION, BY
John MacQueen

EDINBURGH
at the University Press

∗

© J. MacQueen 1970
Edinburgh University Press
22 George Square, Edinburgh
North America
Aldine Publishing Company
529 South Wabash Avenue, Chicago 60605
85224 156 9
Library of Congress
Catalog Card Number 79-92290
Printed in Great Britain by
W. & J. Mackay & Co Ltd, Chatham

PREFACE

In this book I have tried to make a study of the development of the love lyric, and more particularly of the courtly love lyric, in Scotland during the fifteenth and sixteenth centuries. I have stopped at the Reformation, partly because the study depends so much on the Bannatyne MS, which was completed in 1568, and partly because the Reformation made so many changes of general emphasis in Scottish literature and culture. One fact which does emerge clearly is that, during the reign of James V and Mary, the Chapel Royal at Stirling was a very important centre of literary and musical activity. The major figure is Alexander Scott, and I hope that the book will go some way towards establishing his significance not only as poet and musician, but as typifying much of the intellectual and artistic history of a time when Scotland underwent the most profound changes in her history.

For permission to use some of the material in this book, I am grateful to the Trustees of the National Library of Scotland, Edinburgh University Library, the Scottish Record Office, the Council of the Scottish Text Society, Messrs Oliver and Boyd and the Scottish Gaelic Text Society. I have been greatly helped by my friends and colleagues, especially Mr A. J. Aitken, Professor William Beattie, Miss Beth Brown, Miss Nan V. Dunbar, Dr McDonald Emslie, Mr J. S. Ritchie, Dr Grant Simpson, Mr A. R. Turnbull and Mrs Angela West. My wife has kept a keen eye on the book as it developed. The book owes a great deal to the comments of classes at the University of Edinburgh and at Macalester College, St Paul, Minnesota, U.S.A. Any errors are, of course, entirely my own responsibility.

J.M.
School of Scottish Studies
University of Edinburgh, October 1969

> Quhair is the blythnes that hes bein
> bayth in burgh and landwart sein,
> amang lordis and ladyis schein,
> daunsing, singing, game and play?
> Bot now I wait nocht quhat thai mein :
> all mirrines is worne away.

SIR RICHARD MAITLAND of Lethington's comment on the 1560s in Scotland needs little justification. He wrote during the troubled personal reign of Queen Mary and in the midst of the Reformation, a movement historically inevitable, no doubt, however far the social and artistic consequences went towards destroying Scottish culture and civilization. Maitland (1496–1586) was a statesman and poet of some distinction, now best remembered for the manuscript anthology[1] (*c.* 1570–*c.* 1586) from which the opening quotation is taken, and which is preserved in the library of Magdalene College, Cambridge. His motives as a compiler were probably mixed. He was certainly proud of the accomplishment of Scottish letters, but almost equally certainly he shared an additional impulse with his younger contemporaries and fellow-collectors, George Bannatyne[2] (1545–*c.*1608) and the musician Thomas Wode, Vicar of St Andrews (ob. 1592)—the impulse to preserve something of an already suppressed culture which they felt to be in danger of complete disappearance. Perhaps because the Reformation had a more instant effect on music, the sense of a lost,

richer past is particularly strong in Wode, not least
in the note which he added to the treble part of the
canticle *Si quis diligit me*,[3] telling how Francis Heggie,
'ane noveice in the abbay of Sanctandrous' before
1547 added this fifth part to the four-part setting
composed about 1530 by David Peebles (*c.*1510–
1579), a canon of the same Augustinian house. One
notices how Wode links Peebles and Heggie to the
great figures of their own epoch, James v and the
English musician, Dr Robert Fayrfax:

> 'Now yee knaw that this is the fyft pairt maid to
> the four as David Pables first set it and presentit
> the sam to king Jamis the fyft quha wes ane
> musitian him selft; he had ane singular gud eir
> and culd sing that he had never seine before, bot
> his voice wes rawky and harske. I have said in ane
> of thir buks that musik will pereishe, and this
> buke will shaw you sum resons quhy. We se be
> experiance that craft nor syence is not learnit bot
> to the end he may leive be it quhen he hes the
> craft or science; and if Doctor Farfax wer alive
> in this cuntry, he wald be contemnit and pereise
> for layk of mentinance; and sa of neid force it man
> dikeay.'

Wode's primary concern was church music rather
than secular song, but one cannot miss the sub-
stantial general difference between the culture of the
period which preceded the Reformation and that
which followed. Abundant evidence survives to
show the sheer mass of song familiar in the Scotland
of the fifteenth and sixteenth centuries.[4] The
accounts both of the Lord Treasurer and of the

burghs contain many references. Sang sculis existed
in many of the burghs. Those were primarily
ecclesiastical, but secular music has always had a
tendency to encroach on church music, and some
masters of sang sculis are known to have composed
secular pieces. The majority of Scottish composers,
indeed, were churchmen. The technicalities of
musical theory figure prominently and functionally
in the *Orpheus and Eurydice* of Robert Henryson[5]
(?*c*.1420–*c*.1490). William Dunbar[6] (*c*.1460–*c*.
1513) talks of the 'Musicianis, menstralis and mirrie
singaris' in the court of James IV. Gavin Douglas
(*c*.1475–1522) is as knowledgeable as Henryson on
matters of musical theory[7] and includes two elaborate love-songs in his *The Palice of Honour*[8] (1501).
Thirty-eight songs are listed in *The Complaynt of
Scotlande*[9] (1549), while at least thirty of *The Gude
and Godlie Ballatis*,[10] which may have been published
before 1549, are, or have the appearance of being,
adaptations of Scottish and English secular songs for
more or less spiritual purposes.

Nor is the surviving music of the period either
entirely anonymous, or a matter merely of folk-
tunes.[11] The re-foundation of the Chapel Royal at
Stirling by James IV in 1501 stimulated composers of
art-music who came to include such formidable
names as Robert Carver of the Augustinian abbey at
Scone (1491–*c*.1550), Robert Johnson of Duns,
whose dates are uncertain, but who was an approx-
imate contemporary of Carver and spent much of
his life in England, sir John Fethy (?1480–*c*.1570),
who was poet as well as composer, and Andrew
Blackhall (1536–1609), who before the Reformation

was a canon of the Augustinian abbey of Holyrood, but who became a Presbyterian minister, and spent the greater part of his life at Musselburgh near Edinburgh. (The last three all wrote music for secular lyrics.)

In a few years much of this had changed. The beginnings of the collapse may be studied in the poetry of Sir David Lindsay (*c.* 1490–1555), especially in *Ane Satyre of the Thrie Estaitis*,[12] a play which was certainly performed in the 1550s, parts of which, however, may have been written, if not actually performed, as early as the middle 1530s. *Ane Satyre* is one of the most developed specimens of the Morality Play now extant, and it is clear from direct and indirect evidence that it must have been produced with considerable splendour in terms of decor and music. Earlier miracle and morality plays sometimes make striking use of musical resources: one might particularly notice the use of song in the *Prima* and *Secunda Pastorum* of the Wakefield Cycle. Lindsay, at least in his opening scenes, takes the process further. In the latter part of the play the relationship between text and music is scarcely organic. When, for instance, the herald Diligence gives the order,

> Menstrell, blaw up ane brawll of France,
> let se quha hobbils best,
> (4623–4)

he is merely providing the conventional indication that harmony has been restored and the action of the play is over. At the beginning, however, the situation is different. Music and song are related— in caricature perhaps of the liaison between Margaret

Erskine, Lady Lochleven, and James v—to the figure of Lady Sensualitie who seduces the young King Humanitie. It is by means of a song to Venus that Sensualitie and Humanitie are brought together. Solace, one of the royal attendants, has already turned the king's thoughts towards a mistress before the entrance of Lady Sensualitie with her servants Hamelines and Danger, who are immediately joined by Fund-jonet. Their duty is to sing a song to Dame Venus, and it is this song which rouses the king to send Wantonnes, Placebo and Solace as his ambassadors to Sensualitie.

Later in the play, the interval between the dismissal of Gude-counsall and the arrival of Veritie is filled by another of Sensualitie's songs. The stage-direction at this point reads: 'Heir sall the Ladies sing ane sang, the King sall ly doun amang the Ladies and then Veritie sall enter.' It is here, in fact, that Humanitie is lulled into the allegorical sleep which continues with no more than a minor interruption until the turning point of the play, the arrival of Correctioun:

Get up, sir King, ye haif sleipit aneuch
  into the armis of Ladie Sensual
    (1693–4)

For Lindsay, it is clear, one kind of song serves as a dramatic emblem of sexual and general moral laxity, and it is equally clear that what he has in mind is the courtly love lyric. (It is also possible that he may have particularly associated the lyric with the Erskine family, a point which, as will emerge later, may not be entirely without significance.) From

The Historie of Squyer William Meldrum[13] it is easy to
see that Lindsay was sufficiently familiar with the
conventions of courtly love to use them to humorous
as well as serious effect. In the play, Sensualitie is
the bastard daughter of Venus—Venus Pandemos,
that is to say, as she had previously been represented
in the *Roman de la Rose* and Chaucer's *Parlement of
Foulis*:

> Luifers awalk, behauld the fyrie spheir,
> behauld the naturall dochter of Venus:
> behauld luifers this lustie Ladie cleir
> the fresche fonteine of Knichtis amorous.
> repleit with joyis dulce and delicious:
> or quha wald mak to Venus observance?
> In my mirthfull chalmer melodious,
> thair sall thay find all pastyme and pleasance.
> (271-8)

When Lindsay thus equates 'mirthful' music with
sensuality in terms of a parody of the language
of courtly love, he assumes at least one part of the
traditional doctrine that there exists a necessary
relationship, good or bad, between music and conduct. He follows at some distance the Plato who
wished to ban poets and musicians from his Republic
because of the possibly evil effect of their art on
public and private morals.

Nor is he alone in his belief that such a relationship existed. Henryson, for instance, in the passage
from *Orpheus and Eurydice* to which I have already
referred, had illustrated the reverse process. The
sensually fallen Orpheus recovers his full power of
reason by attuning himself to the abstract harmony

of the spheres, a recovery emblematically expressed
by the terms of medieval musical theory which
stand at the furthest remove from the expression of
passion:

> Thair leirit he tonis proportionat,
> as duplare, triplare and epitritus,
> emiolius, and eik the quadruplait,
> epogdous rycht hard and curius.
>   (226–9)

In Lindsay, however, the ultimate emphasis comes
to fall on the corruptive rather than the redemptive
power of music, and it was because his attitude, or a
harsher development of it, came to dominate Scotland, that music and poetry were reduced to the
straits lamented by Thomas Wode.

THE MOST DEPRESSING aspect of this collection
is thus that it illustrates some stages of the death,
even the murder, of a tradition. But that is not the
only aspect. The tradition by then had already lasted
in Scotland for considerably more than a century: it
happens that the first two lyrics written by a Scot
and included here were composed about 1430 by
James I (1406–37) as part of his *Kingis Quair*,[14] and
it is at least possible that others, now lost, had been
composed still earlier. The first and oldest poem in
the book is the *Canticus Troili* from Book I of
Chaucer's *Troilus and Criseyde* (*c*.1385), a Scottish
version of which Bannatyne had the good sense to
include in his anthology. Again, the first 21 lines of
the *Canticus Troili* form 'a fairly close rendering of
Petrarch's sonnet 88 (In Vita), "S'amor non è"',[15]

and Petrarch is the ultimate source from which derives most Western European love poetry of the later fourteenth, fifteenth and sixteenth centuries. Recent scholarship[16] has emphasized the importance of Chaucer, and more particularly the *Troilus and Criseyde*, for the development of the English lyric. Bannatyne's inclusion of a piece which is at once Petrarchan and Chaucerian shows how clear an insight he had for the poetic tradition represented by Part IV of his anthology.

Less often emphasized is the importance of the court poetry of John Lydgate (*c.* 1370–1450). Bannatyne, apparently in ignorance of the fact that he was doing so, included a lyrical extract from *The Temple of Glas.*[17] Insight failed him only when he omitted to represent the love poetry of James I which seems almost as important as that of Chaucer or Lydgate for the general development of the Scottish lyric. This importance results partly from the difference of tone between the Scottish and the English authors. It is difficult to say anything about the poetic *persona* of Lydgate; Chaucer usually adopts that of the detached narrator, capable of sympathetic and imaginative involvement, but equally of ironic or theological withdrawal. The unique quality of the *Troilus and Criseyde* is the apparent imaginative identification at narrative climaxes of the narrator with Troilus. Despite its length, *Troilus and Criseyde* is the nearest approach to a fully lyrical narrative ever written by Chaucer. The poem ends, however in the affirmation of an order which reduces passionate love between man and woman to insignificance; by this, far more than by the portrayal of Criseyde's faithlessness, the poem is the heresy against the doctrines of the God of Love which is denounced in the prologue to *The Legend of Good Women*.[18]

The *persona* adopted by James is quite different; the narrator of the *Kingis Quair* tells his own story with the detachment only of a mature man looking back on the events of his youth. The entire poem is set in the first person singular. Third-person narrative in other words, qualifies and ultimately overthrows the lyricism of the *Canticus Troili*: the first-person lyricism of the *Kingis Quair* is unmodified by such externals, and remains in full accordance with the eventual philosophic position reached by James when he is accepted into the cosmic dance of love. This singleness of effect and intention characterizes some of the best love poetry of the sixteenth century.

The incidentals of the poem also contribute to the development of the tradition. One of the two songs here included is addressed to Venus (as was the first of Lady Sensualitie's songs), and adopts the terminology of the religion of love; the other is addressed to the lady in terms of feudal bondage and loyalty. Formally, the latter is also an address to the poet's heart. None of this is original to James: even the most unusual lines in the songs:

> Folow thy hevin! quho suld be glad bot thou
> that suich a gyde to folow has undertake?
> Were it throu hell, the way thou noght forsake!

reads almost like an effective, if distorted, reminiscence of Dante's journey under Virgil's guidance through hell and purgatory before he is reunited with Beatrice on the border of heaven. More individually important (and almost certainly derived from Lydgate's *Temple of Glas*[19]) is the introduction by Venus of Good Hope as the lover's guide:

> Bot, for the way is uncouth unto thee,
> there as hir dwelling is and hir sojurne,
> I will that Gude Hope servand to thee be,
> your alleris frend, to let the to murn,
> be thy condyt and gyd till thou returne,
> and hir[20] besech, that sche will, in thy nede,
> hir counsele geve to thy welefare and spede.
>   (785–91)

Good Hope reappears in many later love poems, for instance Dunbar's *Beauty and the Prisoner*,[21] or the lively 'Quhen I think on my lady deir'[22]:

> Then is thair non to confort me
> quhen I am standand in that stage:
> suppois I wer in point till de,
> thair is nocht wrey in wardlie wrege
> to rug me then out of that rege:
> than cumis Gud Hoip with lachand cheir
> and biddis me lat all sorrowis swage,
> quhen I think on my lady deir.

THE *Kingis Quair* probably dates from about 1430, and despite its obvious importance, one might be inclined to feel that it is not typical of the poetry of the fifteenth, as opposed to the sixteenth, century in Scotland. Dunbar, for instance, writing the 'Lament for the Makaris'[23] at the beginning of the sixteenth century, singles out one among his predecessors as a poet of love—Mersar, who was dead by about 1508, and of whose poetry several specimens have sur-

vived. Dunbar speaks admiringly of his poetry.
Death

>   hes reft Merseir his endite,
> that did in luf so lifly write,
> so schort, so quyk, of sentence hie.

Not much of Mersar's poetry has survived, and it
may be that Dunbar's third line should have served
as a warning, but it is still something of a shock to
come upon Mersar's 'lively' writing on love:[24]

> Allace! so sobir is the micht
> of wemen for to mak debait
> incontrair menis subtell slicht,
> quhilk ar fulfillit with dissait;
> with tressone so intoxicait
> ar mennis mowthis at all houris,
> quhome in to trest no woman wait:
> sic perrell lyis in paramouris.

If this poem is compared to another[25] by a poet
whom Dunbar also mentions, John Clerk, one might
gain the impression that the detached, moralizing
approach characterizes all Scottish love-lyrics of the
later fifteenth century:

> Thocht luve be grene in gud curage,
> and be difficill till assuage,
> the end of it is miserie.
> Misgovernit youth makis gowsty age.
> Forbeir ye than, and lat it be.

Indeed, there is little in the poetry actually extant
and certainly belonging to the fifteenth century to
suggest the existence in Scotland of any other form

of the love-lyric. Several passages do exist, however, which at least suggest that the general European tradition was maintained.

The Avowis of Alexander is a Scots translation of a late offshoot of the *Roman d'Alixandre*, *Les Voeux du Paon*, composed about 1310 by Jacques de Longuyon. It is preserved in a unique copy, printed in Edinburgh about 1580 by Alexander Arbuthnet, Printer to the King's Majesty, as part of the work now known as *The Buik of Alexander*.[26] The colophon proves that the translation was certainly in existence by 1438:

> And ye may alsweill, gif ye will,
> do the gude and have loving,
> as quhylum did this nobill King,
> that yit is prysed for his bounte,
> the quhether thre hundreth yeir was he
> before the time that God was borne
> to save our saullis, that was forlorne.
> Sensyne is past ane thousand yeir,
> four hundreth and threttie thair-to neir,
> and aucht and sumdele mare, I wis.
>   (Epilogue, 30–9)

The date seems definite enough, although the editor argued with some plausibility that the translation is in fact the work of John Barbour (*c.* 1320–1395).

In the prologue,[27] the translator makes use of the convention that he has written only to assuage the pangs of love—a love which is unmistakeably courtly, and which is expressed in terms which recall those of the love-lyric. The prologue, in other

words, is written for an audience which the author
expected to be thoroughly conversant with the
themes—May, the revival of Nature, the lover's
hopeless passion—characteristic of the lyric, an
audience too which was necessarily one primarily of
Scots. The romance itself presupposes an audience
which was as much concerned with the fine details
of love-making, the gay science, as with battle and
adventure. 'Venus chalmer' is the scene of the love
debates:

> Thay that war left quhen he was gane,
> on silkin carpets sat doun ilkane,
> that strouit war with sindry floures
> wele savorand, of sere coloures.
> Amang thame made thay play and gamyn,
> to solace and to sport thame samyn.
> Thare was demandis and fare answeris,
> enquestis, greting and prayers
> of amouris and his worshep all,
> and of the gude thairof micht fall.
> Thay bourded and gamed fast;
> thare speche ordaned thay at last.
> To 'The King that suld nocht le'
> thay cheisit Betys, and hecht trewlie
> and swore that he suld richteous be
> quhill he was in his majeste.
> Than Idorus of rashes and strais
> full fetasly ane croun sho mais.
> Sho crounit him full courtesly,
> and sat doun sone in cumpany.
>   (2169–88)

I have ventured to treat the reply given by Betys to

a love-question posed by Bauderane as itself a lyric.[28]

If 1438 is accepted as the date at which the translation was completed, it would seem reasonable to suppose that it was begun during the reign of James I, who was murdered in 1437, that James's courtiers formed the audience for which it was intended, and that some at least of them were sympathetic towards poetry of this kind.

Equally obviously in the direct tradition is the anonymous *Lancelot of the Laik*,[29] a long fragmentary romance based on parts of the anonymous thirteenth century French prose *Lancelot del Lac*. The poem consists of a prologue, setting out the author's reasons for writing, and the three books which contain the body of the narrative. The reasons resemble those of the translator of *The Avowis of Alexander*. The author is a victim of hopeless love, and writes not so much to comfort himself as to bring his plight to the notice of his lady, whom he has loved for three years. Lancelot's passion for the Queen, that is to say, is probably to be regarded as in some sense a projection of his own.

The prologue is written in terms of the dream vision convention, and imitates Chaucer's prologue to *The Legend of Good Women*, notably in the emphasis which it lays on the daisy, Queen Alcestis:

> Thar was the flour, thar was the quen Alphest,
> rycht wering being of the nychtis rest,
> unclosing gane the crownel for the day.
> (57–9)

The daisy symbolizes his lady:

> Thar was the garding with the flouris ourfret,
> quich is in posy fore my lady set,
> that hire Represent to me oft befor,
> and thane also.
>   (71–4)

His lady's name, all this is probably to say, was
Margaret, and there is a double suggestion that she
was a queen.

All this fits well enough with the idea, so much
emphasized by Mr Stevens and Mr Southall,[30] that
the poetry of courtly love often bears an intimate
relationship to the realities of courtly life. One may
even venture a little further. Book II consists largely
of the advice on good government given to Arthur
by his adviser, the clerk Maister Amytans. This
passage, it has been convincingly suggested,[31] refers
directly to conditions in Scotland during the reign
of James III (1460–1488), and was intended to come
to the king's notice. If this is accepted, it might
seem reasonable to suppose that the hypothetical
Queen Margaret, for whom the poem was written,
is the same as James III's queen, Margaret of Den-
mark, whom he married in 1468, and that the convention of the dream vision poem has been used to
dignify what in fact is an appeal on the part of the
poet for some kind of patronage. The possibility
remains, even if Alcestis represents, not the queen
but 'ane howir callit the Dæsie', for whose sake,
according to Bishop Leslie in the first draft of his
Historie of Scotland,[32] James was willing 'to contemne
his wyfe, sa worthie a woman'.

More important for our immediate purposes is the

fact that *Lancelot of the Laik* contains specific evidence
that the courtly love lyric was familiar to the author
and his contemporaries. He writes a romance, for
instance, rather than a lyric, because lyrics are so
familiar as to have become trite—or so at least he is
told by 'A birde, that was as ony lawrare gren', who
appears to him in his dream as a messenger from the
God of Love:

> And, for thir sedulis and thir billis are
> so generall, and ek so schort at lyte,
> and sume (?sune) of thaim is lost the appetit,
> sum trety schall yhoue for thi lady sak,
> that uncouth is, als tak one hand and mak.
> (142–6)

'Thir sedulis and thir billis' are courtly love lyrics
of the kind which figure so prominently in Mr R.H.
Robbins's *Secular Lyrics of the XIV and XV Centuries*,[33] and which make up the bulk of the fourth
part of Bannatyne's anthology. Mr Robbins, for
instance, prints a lyric, the final stanza of which
begins:

> Go, litill bill, with all humblis
> unto my lady, of womanhede the floure,
> and saie hire howe newe Troiles lithe in distrez—

and even in the 1560s Darnley was able to begin the
final stanza of a poem:

> Schaw, schedull, to that sweit
> my pairt so permanent,
> that no mirth quhill we meit
> sall caus me be content.

The first book of *Lancelot of the Laik* itself contains a
courtly love lyric,[34] and the evidence of the prologue
that such lyrics were abundantly popular may be
supplemented by the evidence of John Clerk, who
says in the second stanza of the poem already quoted:

> Sa mony ar thair ladeis treitis
> with triumphand amowres balleitis,
> and dois thair bewteis pryis so he,
> that I find not bot daft consaitis
> to say of luve. Bot lat it be—

and by the fact already noted that Gavin Douglas
includes two accomplished specimens of the genre
in his *Palice of Honour*, completed in 1501.[35]

One might even go further. 'Billis' and 'sedulis'
are alternative names for a single literary form—the
love poem cast in the form of a letter to the beloved,
which often enough includes a request for a reply in
kind. Many English examples are to be found in Mr
Robbins's anthology—indeed, he comments[36] that
'the love epistle is the main conventional form during
the fifteenth century', and devotes an entire section
to poems of this kind. Part IV of Bannatyne's anthology might have provided several other instances.
Some are certainly later than the fifteenth century—
that by Darnley, for instance, which has already
been quoted, and others by Alexander Scott and
Bannatyne himself. In each of those, however, there
is at best a perfunctory nod to the form, and no hint
appears that an answer is expected. One or two of
the anonymous poems exploit the convention to a
much greater degree. Such are 'Fresche fragrent
flour of bewte soverane', and 'Fairweill, my Hairt',

both of which I have grouped as possible work of the later fifteenth century.[37]

BY THE EARLY sixteenth century there is positive evidence that some English love-lyrics were familiar in Scotland. 'Allace depairting, grund of wo'[38] is based on two English poems, the first a stanza set to music in Ashmole MS 191 of the middle fifteenth century:[39]

Alas, departyng ys ground of woo!
    oþer songe can y not synge.
but why part y my lady fro,
    syth love was caus of our metyng?
    þe bitter teris of hir wepyng
        myn hert hath pershid so mortaly,
    þat to the deth hit wil me bryng,
        but yf y se hir hastily.

The remaining stanzas are based on the first three stanzas of a four-stanza poem found in Rawlinson MS C.813 of the early sixteenth century:[40]

Farewell now my lady gaye,
    farewell floure most freshest of hew,
farewell sapher yn all assey,
    farewell harte of whyte & blewe,
    farewell kynde, curteyse & trewe,
        farewell woman withowten any evyll,
    farewell þe cumlyst þat ever I knewe—
        I take my leve agaynst my wyll.

farewell now my derlyng dere
    farewell most wysyst & womanly,

farewell my love from yere to yere,
  farewell byrall bryghtest of blee,
  farewell kynde, curteys & free,
    farewell þat may me save & spyll;
  how-ever I fare, well fare ye—
    I take my leve agaynst my wyll.

farewell goodly grond of grace,
  farewell þe well of worthynes,
farewell my comforth yn every case,
  farewell my helpe ferthe of dystresse,
  farewell my werrour from all sykenes,
    farewell my lady of voyce soo shryll,
  farewell nurter & all gentylnesse—
    I take my leve ageynst my wyll.

This *contaminatio* probably results from the fact that
one English poem had a tune, the other a refrain,
and both a common metrical and stanzaic structure.
The Scottish adaptor has combined the two, re-
writing the first stanza to introduce the refrain,
while preserving the first line as an indication of the
tune. Otherwise he changes for the sake of metrical
regularity, or to make the lady more of a type-figure,
a 'pattern'. Thus, he extends the use of the generaliz-
ing definite article in 'Fairweill the saiffar of assay, /
fairweill the hart of quhyt and blew'; he changes the
more homely 'Farewell floure most freshest of hew' to
'Fairweill, fegour most fresch of hew'. In general, he
removes familiar or coloquial touches. 'My derling
dere' becomes 'my richt fair lady deir', and 'kynde,
curteys and free' becomes 'leill lady liberall and fre'
(the latter perhaps also to avoid the near repetition
of 'kynd, curtas and trew' from the previous stanza).

Three lines particularly offended him:

> farewell my helpe ferthe of dystresse,
> farewell my werrour from all sykenes,
>   farewell my lady of voyce soo shryll.

Those became the much more general:

> Fairweill the hoip of steidfastnes:
> fairweill the rute of my distres:
> fairweill the luffar trew and still.

The familiar language of the fourth stanza perhaps caused him to omit it entirely.

The Scottish reviser is in general the more self-consciously sensitive to verbal levels and meanings. Regularity, correctness and decorum are his main concerns in altering, 'improving', the English songs.

THE IMPORTANCE of music for lyric poetry has already been emphasized, and when in the course of the sixteenth century it becomes more possible to provide biographical details of individual authors, the importance of professional musicians as writers of words as well as music becomes more and more obvious. Poems nos. XXIII and XXIV of this collection, for instance, are the work of sir John Fethy (?1480–*c*.1570). The late C.S. Lewis made an appreciative, but somewhat oblique, reference to him in his volume of *The Oxford History of English Literature*:[41] 'It must not be supposed,' he says, 'that Dunbar dominates the minor poets completely. In the beautiful lyric by "Fethe" or Fethy (Bannatyne CCCIX) the poignancy of the refrain "Cauld, cauld culis the lufe that kendillis our het" depends on a quality of rhythm which is quite unlike Dunbar's.' The difference of rhythm is certainly related to the fact, which Lewis does not seem to have recognized, that Fethy was a musician and composer of distinction. Thomas Wode has several notes about him,[42] as for instance to the treble part of 'Shir Jhone Futhies Sang of Repentance': 'I call this man Shir Jhone that he might be knawin, for he wes a papeist priest, and the first trim organeist that ever wes in Scotland'. In the fifth book he notes that the song was 'composit be Shir Jhone Futhy, bayth letter and note', and adds, 'This man wes the first organeist that ever brought in Scotland the curious new fingering and playing on organs, and yit it is mair nor three score yeiris since he cum hame. This is written I. M., V.C., fourscore and XII'. Wode, that is to say, wrote in 1592, and Fethy introduced his new technique in or about 1530. By the middle 1540s Fethy had established himself as a canon of the Chapel Royal of Stirling. In January 1542 the Accounts of the Lord High Treasurer of Scotland record[43] the granting of liveries to 'Schir Johnne Fethyis childer that plays on the viols', probably in return for their services at court during the festivals of Yule and Uphaliday—Christmas and Epiphany. The entry may indicate that Fethy was then in charge of the six boy clerics of the Chapel Royal. By 1545 the connection is certainly established, for in that year he is first mentioned[44] as Chantour (Precentor) of the Chapel Royal, and until the end of his life this remained his usual designation. Other posts, however, came his way: in 1544 he was master of the Aberdeen Sang Scule.[45] There he enjoyed little success: by 13 July 1546, he had effectively given up control of the school to his deputy, John Black, singer.[46] By 1551 he was master of the choir school of Edinburgh, a post which he held until 1568, when he renounced and gave it over to Edward Henderson.[47] He was then a prebend of the choir of St Giles' Kirk in Edinburgh.

As Chantour of the Chapel Royal, Fethy was also person (rector) of St Mary Kirk of the Lowes in Ettrick Forest, a benefice annexed since 1501 to the Chapel Royal. On 12 May 1556, a priest, sir Peter Cranstoun of the Lugehill, became tacksman to sir John Fethy and sir William Myretoune (treasurer of the Chapel Royal) for their parts of St Mary Kirk of the Lowes for the term and space of three years from Lammas 1556.[48] When Fethy made this arrangement, he must have been in some ignorance of conditions in Ettrick Forest, for on 16 April 1557, 200 persons (most of them Scotts), armed in warlike manner, came to the church of St Mary of the Lowes, broke up the doors thereof, and searched for sir Peter Cranstoun therein for his slaughter, upon ancient feud and forethought felony.[49] Apparently they did not find him, for on 16 December 1558, Fethy gave a deed of acquittance to sir Peter Cranstoun.[50] At Lammas 1559 or 1560, the tack was taken up by the laird of Cranstoun, Sir William Cranstoun of that Ilk, but in a somewhat grudging spirit, if one may judge by an entry which Fethy made in the Books of Assumption of Thirds of Benefices, probably before 1 August 1561. Under a note that Fethy's part of St Mary Kirk of the Lowes was presently set by him in assedation to the laird of

Cranstoun for three score pounds Scots money by year, Fethy adds 'and I gat nevir penny payment fra the said laird sen his enteres, quhilk wes at Lambmes wes a yeir by past, and hes na uthir thing to live on, and thairfor protestis for lettres for payment. Sic subscribitur Sir Johnne Fethie with my hand.'[51] It is perhaps as a consequence that Fethy next leased his emoluments to the Cranstouns' enemies, the Scotts: on 20 March 1563, Walter Scott of Branxholme and Dame Jonet Betoun, relict of umquhile Sir Walter Scott of Branxholme, knight, took out a lease for the term and space of three years.[52]

Fethy was now growing old, and by 1566 it was fully established that sir George Gray was to succeed him as Chantour of the Chapel Royal.[53] On 12 August 1566, those two, together with sir George Ross, the treasurer, and sir James Castellaw, the preceptor to the bairnis, leased their emoluments to the Earl of Bothwell,[54] who married Queen Mary a year later. Bothwell had already made his entrance at Lammas, 1566, and his tack was for a period of five years. As has been noted, Fethy was still alive in 1568, but he must have been dead, at latest, by 1570.

Fethy's career suggests that the 'Clappertoun' to whom Maitland attributes 'Way worth maryage for ever mair'[55] is to be identified with sir George Clapperton, a priest who became sub-dean of the Chapel Royal in 1535.[56] Clapperton first appears on record as a prebendary of Trinity collegiate church, Edinburgh, in 1531. The incident recorded by John Knox in *The History of the Reformation in Scotland*[57]

probably occurred not long after his presentation to
Stirling:

> 'But so fearful it was then to speak any thing
> against priests, that the least word spoken against
> them, yea, albeit it was spoken in a man's sleep,
> was judged heresy; and that was practised upon
> Richard Carmichael, yet living [i.e., in 1566] in
> Fife, who being young, and a singer in the Chapel
> Royal of Stirling, happened in his sleep to say,
> "The devil take away the priests, for they are a
> greedy pack." He, therefor accused by sir George
> Clapperton, Dean of the said Chapel, was com-
> pelled therefor to burn his bill.'

From 1538 to 1542 Clapperton was Maister Elimos-
inar to the King's Grace. In 1540 he became Provost
of Trinity Church, Edinburgh, a post which he held
until 1566. In 1564 he was still sub-dean of the
Chapel Royal. He died in 1574, and his testament
shows that he was then a Protestant.[58]

Another poet, this time a layman, who may have
had connections with the Chapel Royal, is the Steill
who wrote 'Lanterne of lufe and lady fair of hew'
(no. XXVIII of the present collection). He is probably to be identified with the George Steel (?1510–
1542) who appears in the Treasurer's accounts
between 1527 and 1542, and who may have been a
groom of the chamber. In 1527 he received a yearly
pension of £40. He seems to have been something
of a specialist in cloth and tapestry. In February
1538, for instance, he was sent to Flanders to bring
home tapestries. In 1539 and 1541 he received cloth
from the king to be made into coats for individual

children of the Chapel Royal. In 'The Complaint and Publict Confessioun of the Kingis Auld Hound, callit Bagsche', David Lindsay mentions Steel as the man who brought to court Bawte, the dog who supplanted Bagsche in the king's affection:

> I rew the race that Geordie Steill
> brocht Bawte to the kingis presence:
> I pray God lat him never do weill
> sen syne I gat na audience,
> for Bawte now gettis sic credence
> that he lyis on the kingis nycht goun,
> quhare I perforce for my offence
> man in the clois ly like ane loun
> (17–24)

As the story of his death shows, Steel was a fervent, if untheologically minded, Catholic. John Knox's *History of the Reformation in Scotland* is again the source of information: [59]

> 'In his own (James v's) presence, George Steill, his greatest flatterer, and greatest enemy to God that was in his Court, dropped off his horse, and died without word that same day that, in open audience of many, the said George had refused his portion of Christ's Kingdom if the prayers of the Virgin Mary should not bring him thereto.'

MORE IMPORTANT as a poet, though as a musician less important than Fethy, is Alexander Scott, the best of whose lyrics in their humorous, ironic and passionate complexity are scarcely equalled by those of any other known Scottish poet. His

work and his life illustrate almost every point I have
tried to make in the earlier part of this introduction.
He was born, we may guess, somewhere about 1515.
Elsewhere[60] I have tried to show that the authorship of the beautiful lyric 'Lo, quhat it is to luve',
attributed both to Scott and Sir Thomas Wyatt,
more probably belongs to Scott, but that Wyatt
wrote a reply. If that is so, Scott must have written
the poem in the late 1530s or early 1540s (Wyatt
died in 1542), and must also have had some kind of
connection with English court literary circles. The
weaker among Scott's poems:

> Thocht I in grit distress
>   suld de in to dispair,
> I can get no redress
>   of you, my lady fair.
>   Howbeid my time I wair
> alhaill in your schervyce,
>   ye compt nocht of my cair:
> I find you ay so nice—

might almost be taken for sub-standard Wyatt.

In 1540 we have a possible vivid glimpse of the
poet,[61] for in Paris on 26 June of that year Claude
Chorel, clerk of the Palace and captain of the band of
the Knights of the Table Round of the King of the
Basoche, made a contract with Jehan de Laulnay, a
Swiss tambourin player, who lived in the rue
Greneta, and Alexander Scott, a fife player who
lived in the Rue du Temple. No further details are
given, save that de Laulnay and Scott were each to
receive an elaborate plumed livery and 21 *sous
tournois*. It is possible, however, to go a little beyond

the documents. The King of the Basoche was the leader of the official association of clerks of the Palace of Justice in Paris. His empire was divided into chapters, the members of which wore a special uniform and were governed by a captain. 'They assembled at stated times, such as the beginning of July, when they were obliged by statute to present themselves at a *montre*, or general review. On these occasions they performed pantomimes, or *tableaux vivants*, and, as time went on, dialogues, farces and moralities, often written by their own members and usually satirizing the world of the judicature, from which these members were drawn.' (I quote the article in *The Oxford Companion to French Literature*.[62])

It seems pretty certain that Chorel hired de Laulnay and Scott, two foreign-born professional musicians residing in Paris, to take part in the *montre* held at the beginning of July 1540, and as part payment issued them with the livery of his chapter, the Knights of the Table Round. It is no more than a suggestion that Alexander Scott the fife player and Alexander Scott the poet were the same, but at least definite evidence exists that the poet Scott was also a professional musician, and the tone of many among his poems would blend admirably with the festivities of the Basoche. It is conceivable that he was a student (perhaps of music) in Paris who grasped the opportunity to turn an honest penny and at the same time have a little fun.

If Scott was a student in Paris, he was almost certainly supported financially by a Scottish benefice. On 28 February 1539, the Register of the Privy Seal of Scotland records[63] that one Alexander Scott was presented with the prebend of the Chapel Royal at Stirling called Ayr—his rent, that is to say, was the revenue of the parsonage of Ayr which, like that of St Mary Kirk of the Lowes, was annexed to the Chapel Royal. (This implies no more than that he was at least in minor orders—there is no suggestion that he was a priest.) A somewhat complicated line of argument, beginning from the fact that the poet Scott had demonstrable connections with the Erskine family, suggests that this prebendary and the poet were the same. It was in memory of Lord Erskine's eldest son, Robert, the lover of the Queen-dowager, Mary of Guise, that Scott wrote 'The Lament of the Maister of Erskine',[64] a poem which is obviously written to be sung, and for which the musical setting has survived. Erskine was killed at the battle of Pinkie in 1547.

Robert Erskine had been commendator of the Augustinian priory of Inchmahome, situated on an island in the Lake of Menteith, Perthshire, where he was succeeded by his younger brother John, the future Regent Mar. On 12 July 1548, John Erskine granted[65] a canon's portion in his priory to the musician and organist Alexander Scott 'for the decoir of our queir in musik and playing'. Almost certainly, as Dr Durkan[66] has indicated, this musician is to be identified with the poet. It is probably significant, however, that the grant stresses payment to Scott 'alsweill in his absence as presens', for two weeks later, on 23 July,[67] the Queen and the Regent Arran granted a licence 'to oure lovit familiar clerk, Maister Johne Erskin, prior of Inchmaholmo, and with him in service Alexander Scott, persoun of Balmaclellane,

to pass to the partis of France and ony utheris beyond sey in our service, and for doing of his uthir
lefull besynes and erandis as he sall think expedient'.
Erskine's servant must be the same as the organist,
more especially since his designation as parson of
Balmaclellan (in the stewartry of Kirkcudbright)
implies that he was a canon of the Chapel Royal—
Balmaclellan too was one of the benefices annexed
for its upkeep—and so a musician. As it seems un-
likely that in the course of a decade two Alexander
Scotts were members of the Chapel Royal, the poet
and musician is almost certainly to be identified
with the prebendary who in 1539 became parson of
Ayr.

One need only add that in 1547 the young Mary
Queen of Scots had resided under Lord Erskine's
tutelage in the priory of Inchmahome, and that
Erskine's journey to France probably had some connection with the Queen's own departure for France
on 7 August 1548. In the Register of the Privy Seal [68]
the document which follows the one just quoted is a
respite and exemption granted by the Queen to
John, Lord Erskine, the commendator's father, and
Alexander Livingstone, 'for sa mekle as it is thocht
expedient . . . that thai pas instantlie with us to
the realme of France'. Commendator Erskine and
Alexander Scott may well have travelled in the
Queen's company.

The documentary evidence thus far converges on
a poet and musician who by 1547 was parson of
Balmaclellan and Ayr, canon of the Chapel Royal,
canon and organist of Inchmahome, servant of the
Erskine family and in all probability of the Queen,

one too who must have had a fairly thorough
acquaintance with French life at more than one
social level. In the twenty years following, the pattern changed very markedly, although we have
little documentary evidence other than the poems
to explain the alteration. By 1561 Scott had lost, or
given up, the benefices connected with the Chapel
Royal; sir George Gray, who was later to succeed
Fethy as Chantour, was by then parson of Balmaclellan and Mr Robert Dennestoune parson of Ayr. [69]
Scott too had certainly adopted some form of
Protestantism. 'Of May', a poem with distinctly
protestant undertones, belongs to the years between
1555 and 1560[70], and Scott's longest poem, 'Ane
New Yeir Gift to the Quene Mary, quhen scho come
first Hame; 1562',[71] contains some vigorous adverse
criticism of the old church and its clergy. The poem
avoids positive condemnation of the Mass (which
in a congratulatory address to a Catholic queen
would certainly have been tactless) and Scott is as
severe on the behaviour of some members of the
reformation party as that of the Catholic hierarchy.
Unmistakeably, however, the poem is the work of a
Protestant.

This was the period during which differences
between Protestant and Catholic in Scotland came
to a head. George Wishart, the protestant martyr,
had been burned on 1 March 1546, and on 29 May
of the same year Cardinal Beaton was murdered in
revenge. In July 1547, only a few weeks before Queen
Mary's departure for France, the protestant garrison
of St Andrews Castle (John Knox among them)
surrendered. Reforming councils of the Scottish

province of the church were held in 1549, 1552 and 1559. The rebellion of 1559 led to the Reformation of 1560.

Scott's development as an individual corresponds to the general national pattern. His departure from the Chapel Royal may indicate only that he had become a Protestant (compare the story of Richard Carmichael and sir George Clapperton already quoted), but it may also have been affected by more personal happenings. On 21 November 1549, the Register of the Great Seal of Scotland records the legitimization of John Scott and Alexander Scott, full brothers, bastards, natural sons of Alexander Scott, prebendary of the Chapel Royal at Stirling.[72] There is no evidence that Scott was ever in priestly orders and so necessarily a celibate; the legitimization was thus probably *post subsequens matrimonium*— it occurred, that is to say, because Scott had married the mother of his two sons. We have at least one piece of evidence to suggest that Scott actually (and unhappily) married in Bannatyne's remark at the conclusion of 'To luve unluvit',[73] 'Quod Scott, quhen his wife left him'.

Scott is severe on the sexual licence of the pre-Reformation church:

> Bot wyte the wickit pastouris wald nocht mend
> thair vitious leving all the warld prescryvis;
> thai tuke na tent thair traik sould turne till end,
> thai wer sa proud in thair prerogatyvis;
> for wantonnes thay wald nocht wed na wyvis
> nor yit leif chaste, bot chop and change thair
>   cheir;

now, to reforme thair filthy licherous lyvis
God gife thee grace aganis this guid New Yeir.

Thai brocht thair bastardis with the skrufe thai
   skraip
to blande thair blude with barrownis be
   ambitioun;
thai purchest pithles pardonis fra the Paip
to caus fond folis confide he hes fruitioun,
as God, to gif for synnis full remissioun
and saulis to saif frome suffering sorowis seir;
to sett aside sic sortis of superstitioun
God gife thee grace aganis this gude New Yeir.

Thai lost baith benefice and pentioun that mareit
and quha eit flesch on Frydayis was fyrefangit,
it maid na mis quhat madinnis thai miscareit
on fasting dayis, thai wer nocht brint nor hangit;
lieence for luchrie fra thair lord belangit
to gif indulgence, as the devill did leir;
to mend that menye hes samonye mangit
God gif thee grace aganis this guide New Yeir.
   ('Ane New Yeir Gift to the Quene Mary',
   57-80)

Other poems suggest that his own behaviour was
sometimes less high-minded than Scott here tries to
indicate, but the passage does have a fire and urgency
which may mean that his personal feelings were
more than usually involved in his subject matter. In
explanation, it is perhaps cynical to single out one line
—'Thai lost baith benefice and pentioun that mareit'
—but it is certainly noticeable that prebendaries
of the Chapel Royal (witness Fethy) generally

preserved this status to the end of their lives, that after 1549 Scott is nowhere mentioned as a prebendary, and that in 1549 he may well have married. It may, or may not, be relevant that on 6 February 1567, Alexander Scott, younger (one of the poet's two sons), received the canonry and prebendary of the Chapel Royal of Stirling 'callit the half personage and vicarage of the kirk of Quiltoun Secundo' (Coylton in Ayrshire).[74] The appointment might be taken to mean that the elder Alexander Scott had remained on good terms with his former colleagues, or alternatively that after the Reformation they felt able to make him some reparation for the wrong which he had previously suffered. The appointment almost certainly is connected with the poet's previous term of office in the Chapel Royal.

If Scott suffered any hardship, things improved for him before the Reformation of 1560. In the middle 1560s he is twice on record[75] as a canon of Inchaffray, a Perthshire house of Augustinians situated at no enormous distance from Inchmahome and Stirling. In 1565 he was in receipt of Inchaffray pensions totalling £53.13s. 4d. — something which indicates that he must have become a member of the community (presumably as their organist) before the Reformation settlement. By this time he was in fact a man of some wealth. On 2 January 1567, Alexander Scott, musician, purchased Nether Petledie, part of the lands of Balberdie and the lands of Balfour in the Sheriffdom of Fife,[76] and on 10 May 1570, he purchased from Patrick Murray of Newraw, a fellow-canon of Inchaffray, 'all and haill my landis of Tulicandych and Kirklandis of Maderdy—lyand

within the baron of Maderdy within the sheriffdom
of Perth'.[77] (These last had been Inchaffray lands
before the Reformation.) I have already mentioned
that on 6 February 1567, his son Alexander received
the half-parsonage and vicarage of Coylton in
Ayrshire: this may help to explain the fact that on
or about 4 November 1580, Alexander Scott, elder,
musician, Alexander Scott, younger, his son, and
Elizabeth Lindsay, spouse of Alexander Scott,
younger, obliged themselves to pay an annual rent
out of the eight merkland of Penefoidyoch, barony of
Cumnock, baillery of Kyle Stewart, sheriffdom of
Ayr.[78] The rent was to be paid to Harie Stewart,
Appearand of Craigyhall and Dame Jean Ross, Lady
Calder, his spouse. Alexander Scott, younger, died
shortly afterwards. On 10 April 1582, Alexander
Scott, grandson to Alexander Scott, musician, and
son of umquhile Alexander Scott, brother to John
Scott, purchased the lands of Lytill Prestoun, 'lyand
within the lordship of Stow and the sheriffdom of
Edinburgh'.[79] John Scott outlived his father. On 30
July 1583, he obtained a decree as son of umquhile
Alexander Scott for registration of an obligation,
granted on 18 June 1582, by Dene Patrick Murray of
Newraw to the said umquhile Alexander for an
annual rent of £50 to be taken from the lands of
Maderty and Tullycandie.[80] The poet, that is to
say, was still alive on 18 June 1582, but was dead by
30 July 1583. It is probably safe to assume that he
died in the early months of 1583.

Alexander Montgomerie (*c.*1545–1597) refers to
Scott in a sonnet[81] addressed in or about the year
1584 to the English musician and poet, Robert

Hudson, who in 1586 became Master of James
VI's Chapel Royal:

> Ye knaw ill guiding genders mony gees
> and specially in poets. For example,
> ye can pen out twa cuple, and ye pleis,
> yourself and I, old Scot and Robert Semple.
> Quhen we ar dead that all our dayis bot daffis,
> let Christan Lyndesay wryt our epitaphis.

This does not imply that in 1584 Scott was still
alive; 'we' in 'Quhen we ar dead' means 'you,
Robert Hudson, and I, Alexander Montgomerie',
while the adjective 'old' probably indicates that
Scott's death was recent enough for him to be remembered vividly and affectionately. Hudson was a
musician, Montgomerie was not; correspondingly,
Scott was a musician, Semple was not. Semple in
fact was the most outspoken and accomplished
protestant versifier of the 1570s, and it may be
significant that the catholic Montgomerie links
such a name with that of Scott. In Part III of his MS,
Bannatyne groups[82] three poems by Scott with three
by Semple and one by 'Ane Inglisman'—perhaps
Robert Hudson himself. None of those poems however is self-evidently protestant.

One might add in parenthesis that when Montgomerie wrote, Semple had recently endured a term
in jail. On 4 September 1582, George Buchanan of
that Ilk entered into an obligation with James, Earl
of Arran and Dame Elizabeth Stewart, his spouse,
'to enter and deliver Robert Symple, burgess of
Dumbartane, callit utherwys the Maker, quha hes
bein kept be thame for certane crimes quheirof he is

suspectit'. On 23 December, the Earl and his spouse gave an acquittance to Buchanan, notwithstanding he had failed to enter and deliver 'Robert Symple the Poett, committit to the keping of the said Erle and his Spouse by our Soverane Lord'.[83]

It is clear from his work, as well as from the surviving details of his life, that Scott had professional connections with the court and the nobility—connections which may help to explain, for instance, the grave familiarity of tone with which he addresses Queen Mary. The pure love lyrics belong entirely to such a courtly *milieu*. Less self-evident, or at least less often mentioned, is the gradual inclination towards Protestantism suggested by the biographical details, and to some modest extent confirmed by the existence of vernacular translations of the first and fiftieth Psalms attributed to Scott. Those parallel the other protestant translations of the century, most notably those of Wyatt and Surrey.

THE MAJORITY of Scott's poems fall into two main classes; on the one hand, love lyrics and poems about lovers, which would fit well enough into the court of Lindsay's Lady Sensualitie; on the other, moral poems of advice and exhortation, many in condemnation of the practices of lovers and their ladies. Poems of the second group sometimes show traces of Protestantism. It seems likely that the first group, as a whole and on the whole, preceded the second.

It is certainly easy to arrange Scott's poems in an order which suggests some such history. Indeed, it is scarcely necessary to alter the order in which the poems appear in the MS. Some are not so much love poems as detached, cynical, sometimes satiric comments on love and lovers. Consider, for instance, the treatment of women which Scott recommends lovers to adopt in 'It cumis you luvaris to be laill'.[84]

> Defend thair fame, quha evir fyle thame,
> and ay with honest havingis style thame,
> to Venus als suppois ye wile thame,
>   ressoun;
> bot be ye fraudfull and begyle thame,
>   tressoun.
>
> Ye suld considdir or ye taik thame
> that littill service will nocht staik thame;
> get ye ane goldin hour to glak thame,
>   ressoun;
> bot be ye fraudfull and forsaik thame,
>   tressoun.

Particularly noticeable is the way in which Scott exploits the formal qualities of his stanza to give ironic expression to his observation of the hypocrisy and self-contradiction inherent in the practice of courtly love. The poem as a whole depends on an apparent opposition between the first four and the concluding two lines of each stanza, an opposition most strongly present in the one-word rhyming lines, 'ressoun' and 'tressoun', which form a kind of refrain. The third line of each stanza, however, makes it plain that neither word has its ordinary meaning, that courtly lovers use a kind of double-speak which bears little relation to the facts of the situation, but a great deal to the preservation of external appearance. In the stanzas quoted, 'fame', 'honest havingis', 'service' and 'ressoun' are balanced against 'fraudfull' and 'tressoun'; the effect depends on the fact that 'fame' and 'honest havingis' are reconcilable with Venus; 'service' with 'ane goldin hour to glak thame'. The vulgar force of 'glak' (a four-letter word, usually glossed 'trifle with') is particularly striking, especially as it is balanced by the deliberately conventional and colourless 'forsaik thame', the ultimate sin of the courtly convention. The unemphatic and casually dismissive use of the pronoun 'thame' strengthens the total effect.

'Luve preysis but comparesone'[85] moves towards personal involvement, and has a possible external reference discussed below, but it is again primarily the statement of Scott's ironic and anarchic philosophy of love. Earlier poets had often enough worked in terms of the religion of love which parodied the hierarchy of the universal church. Scott went one stage further, and might almost be regarded as a Lollard in the theology of love. (This has a relevance to his probable later development.) One stanza certainly seems to echo the famous question posed almost two centuries before by John Ball and his followers:

Ferme luve for favour, feir or feid,
of riche nor pur to speik suld spair:
for luve to hienes hes no heid,
nor lychtleis lawlines ane air,
bot puttis all personis in compair
this proverb planely for till preve,
that men and wemen, les and mair,
ar cumd of Adame and of Eve.

The consequences are obvious:

> So luvaris lair no leid suld lak,
> a lord to lufe a silly las,
> a leddy als for luf to tak
> ane proper page hir time to pas:
> for quhy as bricht bene birneist bras
> as silver wrocht at all devys,
> and als gud drinking out of glas
> as gold, thocht gold gif grittar prys.

Scott suggests that he regards love as merely appetitive, not only by the phrase 'hir time to pas', but also by the imagery of the last four lines which parallel the enjoyment of love with the use of silver and brass platters for food, gold and glass vessels for drink. And his power of humorous *double entendre* is obvious in the first stanza:

> For luve makis nobill ladeis thrall
> to bassir men of birth and blud;
> so luve garris sobir wemen small
> get maistrice our grit men of gud.

The poem as a whole gains force from Scott's masterly use of alliteration within single lines, or to emphasize syntactic continuity from one line to another.

A few of the genuine love lyrics are poems of happy abandonment to the sensual power of love. Most notable of those is 'Up, helsum hairt',[86] with its somewhat unusual treatment, this time of the feudal imagery of courtly love. Cupid is king; the lover is one of his barons—a heritor whose heritage is the lady's heart, which he holds subject to the payment of token dues—'in blenche ferme for ane sallat every May'. No other service is demanded, he is 'free of all thirlaige'. In the courtly tradition, the love is adulterous:

> I coft hir deir, bot scho fer derrer me,
> quhilk hasard honor, fame, in aventeur,
> committing clene hir corse to me in cure.

The dominant note is joy of possession:

> I knaw no siching, sadnes, nor yit soun,
> walking, thocht, langour, lamentatioun,
> dolor, dispair, weiping, nor jelosye;
> my breist is void and purgit of pussoun;
> I feill no pane, I haif no purgatorye,
> bot peirles, perfytt, paradisall plesour.

This note is rare in the other poems, and even when it occurs, it tends to be qualified by reminiscences of pain. The sequence of beautiful images, for instance, in 'Rycht as the Glass bene thirlit thrucht with bemis'[87] is disturbed by a single line, 'And as the kokatrice keilis with hir sicht', where the suggestion of poison and cruelty alters the balance of the entire poem. 'Quha is perfyte'[88] ends with the same joy of possession as 'Up, helsum hairt', but the structure of the poem turns on the expression and realization of the balance between pain and pleasure in the experience of love. Pleasure is the obverse of pain, and the poet realizes in himself how the two states are united, and how he must keep silence about it afterwards—again, it is an adulterous relationship:

> Albeid I knaw of luvis law
> the plesour and the panis smart,
> yit I stand aw for to furthschaw
> the quiet secreitis of my harte,
> for it may Fortoun raith to do hir body skaith
> quhilk wait that of thame baith I am expert.

The paradoxical synthesis of the final stanza is expressed in what is perhaps one of Scott's most perfect cadences:

> Thair is nocht wie can estimie
> my sorrow and my sichingis sair,
> for so am I done fathfullie
> in favouris with my lady fair,
> that baith our hairtis are ane, luknyt in luvis chene
> and everilk grief is gane for evir mair.

I have several times hinted at the rational, almost philosophic, attitude of mind which shows, for instance, through the gnomic utterances of such a poem as 'Lo, quhat it is to luve' (if that is indeed by Scott), and even through the cynicism of some of the other poems. The same quality is clearly present in 'Quha is perfyte'. Scott not only realizes the conventional paradoxes of love, he attempts to resolve them, to his emotional, if not always his intellectual, satisfaction. He observes as he experiences, and he is never wholly unconscious of the inner dichotomy traditionally expressed in terms of the conflict between wit and will. His wit, however, is a practical one, concerned more with immediate physical experience than abstract reason. One may compare the unusual use of the word 'ressoun' as a refrain in 'It cumis you luvaris to be laill'. This characteristic combines with the tradition of the address to the heart, and may go far to explain the fact that Scott personifies his interior debate, not in terms of wit and will, but in terms of body and heart. For Scott the lyric poet, the body seems the normative, rational part of the human being; the heart is the seat of the unregenerate, irrational will—the will which at the same time is the only part of the human being to possess a freedom which in some sense is genuine, despite the abuse to which it subjects itself.

The concept most closely fits those poems which express the dichotomy at its greatest intensity; poems, that is to say, which deal with the pains rather than the pleasures of love. That is true even of 'The Answeir to the Ballat of Hairtis',[89] a poem which appears to have been written in response to 'Haif hairt in hairt',[90] which in turn must have been addressed to Scott by a woman. The intention of the latter poem is certainly encouraging, but even so, pain is what Scott emphasizes:

It is na gravit hairt in stone,
in silver, gold, nor evir bone,
nor yit ane payntit symlitud;
bot this same verry hairt allone
within my breist of flesch and blude.

Scott gives the conceit a more precise treatment in 'Oppressit hairt, endure'.[91] He addresses his heart throughout:

Perfors tak paciens and dre thy destany.
To lufe but recompens is grit perplexitie.
Of thine adversitie wyt thy self and no mo,
for quhen that thou wes fre, thou wald nocht
     hald thee so—

Bot yit my corps, allace, is wrangusly opprest
be thee in to this cace and brocht to grit wanrest.
Quhy suld it so be drest be thee and daly pynd
quhilk still it ay detest, thy wantoun folich mind?

The most elaborate development of the conceit
appears in two linked poems, 'Hence, hairt, with
hir that most departe' and 'Returne thee, hairt,
hamewart agane'.[92] I take it as self-evident that the
poems are connected, that the first preceded the
second, and that both refer to the same woman.
The two poems follow an identical metrical and
stanzaic pattern, and each is provided with a
refrain. The words of the first were set to music,[93]
and if they ever became popular, it would be easy
and effective for the words of the second to be sung
to the same tune.

It would be surprising, nevertheless, if the passage
of the years had not intruded Reason into the
psychology of Scott's love poems. In a sense, indeed,
Reason had been present there from the beginning.
I have already mentioned the detached cynicism of
the poems which observe rather than participate in
the ritual of love. To an extent, such cynicism is
rational, and it is absent from only a few of Scott's
extant poems. One might even venture a little
further. Notoriously it is risky to postulate a direct
connection between literature and life, and in the

absence of plentiful biographical details it is particularly risky. None the less, it is easy to read Scott's lyrics as recording the effect on a temperament naturally inclined to detachment and cynicism of an unhappy experience of passionate love, an experience which ultimately impelled him towards total rejection and a position from which it was easy for him to adopt some, perhaps all, of the more rigorous beliefs and attitudes of the Reformers.

Relevant here is the extent to which the entire Reformation was a movement towards an apparent rationality.

> Get up, thou sleipis all too lang, O Lord,
> and mak sum ressonabill reformatioun
> (1160–1)

had been the cry of Lindsay's Lady Veritie as Flattrie, Falset and Dissait put her in the stocks, and it is typical of much of the later movement. The dominant note of the middle section of Scott's poem to the Queen on her return is sheer scorn at the follies of the past and the present:

> Thai lute thy liegis pray to stokkis and stanes
> and paintit paiparis, wattis nocht quhat thai
>   meine;
> thai bad thame bek and bynge at deid mennis
>   banes,
> offer on kneis to kis, syne saif thair kin:
> pilgrimes and palmaris past with thame betwene
> Sanct Blais, Sanct Boit, blait bodeis ein to bleir.
> Now, to forbid this grit abuse hes bene,
> God gife thee grace aganis this guid New Yeir.

> Thai tyrit God with tryfillis, tume trentalis,
> and daisit him with daylie dargeis,
> with owklie abitis to augment thair rentalis,
> mantand mort mumlingis mixt with monye leis.
> (81–92)

For Scott, the process was gradual, but an early stage is visible in the final stanzas of 'To luve unluvit': [94]

> Quhattane ane glaikit fule am I
> to slay myself with malancoly
> sen weill I ken I may nocht get hir!
> or quhat suld be the caus and quhy
> to brek my hairt, and nocht the bettir?

> My hairt, sen thou may nocht hir pleis,
> adew, as gud lufe cumis as gais,
> go, chus ane udir and foryet hir.
> God gif him dolour and diseis
> that brekis thair hairt and nocht the bettir!

Scott here is not too far distant from the fabliau attitude of Pandarus in Book v of Chaucer's *Troilus and Criseyde*, but he is at least advising himself rather than someone else.

The adoption of such an attitude may well have occurred at a fairly early date. I have already commented on the relationship between Scott and Wyatt, illustrated generally by the style of Scott's poetry, and in particular by 'A Rondel of Love'. If my argument about this last poem is correct, Scott must have written it at some time prior to Wyatt's death in 1542. The poem offers itself as the product of experience:

> Lo, quhat it is to lufe!
> Lerne, ye that list to prufe,
> be me, I say, that no ways may
> the grund of greif remufe,
> bot still decay, both nycht and day
> Lo, quhat it is to lufe!

For Scott, the most painfully obvious aspect of love is its irrationality, or rather the manic-depressive alternation of rational and irrational which accompanies the passion:

> To lufe and to be wyis,
> to rege with gud advyis,
> now thus, now than, so gois the game,
> incertane is the dyis.
> Thair is no man, I say, that can
> both lufe and to be wyis.

To avoid love entirely, 'fle alwayis frome the snair', is the solution which he suggests.

Reason is opposed to Cupid and triumphs over him in 'Leif, Luve, and lat me leif allone'.[95] 'In June the jem'[96] is a serene and humorous rejection of passionate love couched in a parody of legal terms which would almost fit a 'Lybell of repudie' such as Diomeid sent to Cresseid in Henryson's poem. A few legal phrases—'This present to compile express', 'Gif scho my luve quit clame'—suffice to point the legal style of the poem as a whole, with its carefully balanced clauses and conditions, 'Be scho-', 'Will scho-', 'Quhen scho-', 'Pleis scho-'. Scott makes a few apparently conciliatory gestures, but his rejection remains in all essentials total:

> Quhair power ma not plais,
> adew! without disais;
> als gud luve cumis as gais,
>   or rathir bettir——
>
> Bot gif scho steidfast stand,
> and be not variand,
> I am at hir command—
>   conforme to ressone.

'Ressone', it is obvious from this last stanza, belongs to a range of the spectrum very different from that of 'luve'—and Scott himself is to be the judge in all questions of rationality.

Two poems, both probably late, show Scott's rational cynicism merging into the religious rationalism of the Reformers. In one,[97] the emphasis is on the triumph of wit over will in old age:

> Fra raige of youth the rink hes rune,
> and Ressone tane the man to tune:
> the brukle body than is wune,
> and maid ane veschell new:
> for than thruch grace he is begune
> the well of wisdome for to kune:
> than is his weid of vertew spune
> trest weill this taill is trew.

Reason in old age controls and reconciles body and heart alike, and the vocabulary and phraseology— *veschell new, grace, well of wisdome, weid of vertew*—are at once strongly biblical and strongly Protestant.

'Quha lykis to luve'[98] is interesting in a number of ways. In the first place, a reference to the plague suggests that it may have been written as late as

1568. The manner, secondly, recalls that of 'Lo, quhat it is to luve', but the state of the lover is portrayed in darker and more violent tones. The world he inhabits is self-evidently preposterous:

> Fle thocht he wald, Lufe sall him hald
> within the dungeoun of dispair,
> quhyle hett, quhyle cald, a thousand fald
> his purpois salbe heir and thair:
> he sall hald wisdome vice
> and vertew of no price
> bot as a fule unwyce
>   so sall he fair.

The Old Testament note in the last few lines is palpable, and helps to prepare for the last stanza, which I quote more as illustrating Scott's final position than for any intrinsic merit:

> My brethir deir, we most forbeir
> and fra this sinfull life evaid us.
> Lat Ressoun steir your hairtis inteir
> and nocht thoill lathly lust to leid us,
> quhilk is the verry net
> that Satane for us set
> to caus us quyt foryet
>   the Lord that maid us.

Reason now has, or ought to have, so complete a mastery over the heart that it turns inevitably to God. The Scott who wrote this is very close to the Scott who translated the Psalms:

> Wesche me, and mak my sawle serene
> frome all iniquite that bene,

clenge me of crime and mak me clene
all vycis for to fle.
For my transgressioun haif I sene,
quhilk tormentis me with tray and tene,
and ay my sin forgane mine ene:
Lord God, deliver me.

After this, it is not likely that Scott wrote any more
love poems.

ENOUGH PERHAPS has been said to establish the
complexity of tone and attitude in Scott's poetry, a
complexity, one must admit, which seems to exist
within fairly narrow boundaries. For all that, one
should not forget the existence of the address to
Queen Mary, the satires and the translation of the
Psalms—not to mention 'The justing and debait up
at the Drum, betwix William Adamsone and
Johnie Sym', a poem in the rumbustious central
tradition of Scottish humorous verse. Within those
boundaries, Scott's stylistic equipment is equal to
all the demands he makes on it. His most obvious
gift—a fine control of metre, rhyme, alliteration and
stanzaic form—is probably related to his training as
a musician. Pre-eminently his verse is singable.
Correspondingly, his normal level of diction is
unobtrusively clear and polished, an almost perfect
example of the courtly middle style:

To luve unluvit it is ane pane,
for scho that is my soverane,
sum wantoun man so he hes set hir,
that I can get no lufe agane,
but brekis my hairt, and nocht the bettir.

This habitual easiness of style helps to disguise some of the effects—humorous, ironic, satirical—which Scott achieves, often in swift asides which pass almost before the reader or hearer notices. Some I have already mentioned:

> So luve garris sobir wemen small
> get maistrice our grit men of gud,

or

> Als gud luve cumis as gais—
>   or rathir bettir,

or

> I am at hir command—
>   conforme to ressone.

It is not difficult to find others. A single word— 'Buchone' in the following example[99]—may profoundly affect the meaning of a stanza:

> In May sould men of amouris go
> to serf thair ladeis, and no mo,
> sen thair releis in ladeis lyis;
> for sum may come in favouris so
> to kiss his loif on Buchone wise.

The refrain or the final line of a poem may clash stylistically with the remainder, often with the effect of a sudden, impatient dash of cold water. Even if we ignore the pun on Scott's own name, the final line of 'Luve preysis but comparesone' has this effect:

> Scho may persave sum Inglis throw it.

The vigorous colloquialism of the refrain in 'Returne thee, hairt',

> For feind a crum of thee scho fawis—

has a similar shock effect at the end of the first stanza, a stanza which for the most part has preserved a more decorous linguistic level. The refrain at the same time prepares us for the remainder of the poem and the deliberate stylistic descent found in such words and phrases as 'bestiall' (line 11), 'se quha playis best thair pawis' (line 14), 'lat fillok ga fling hir fill' (line 15), 'a fellone menyie' (line 19), the familiar proper names Meg, Marjorie and Mawis in line 22, and the final couplet:

> And latt hir fallow ane filly fair,
> for feind a crum of thee scho fawis.

No greater contrast of method could be found than between this and its companion poem, 'Hence, hairt, with hir that most departe', which maintains a single stylistic level from first to last.

Scott uses proverbs and proverb-like expressions to similar effect. In terms of rhetorical theory, a proverb might be used for stylistic adornment at any level. Scott tends, however, to use them at a level somewhat beneath that of the remainder of the poem. The effect is sometimes satiric, sometimes even degrading, but it may also heighten the reader's sense of the actuality of the situation described. I have already commented on the effect of the proverbial comparison in 'Luve preysis but comparesone':

This proverb planely for till preve
that men and wemen, les and mair,
ar cumd of Adame and of Eve.

(One might add that it also emphasizes original sin.)
The effect is primarily satirical, as it is in the later

as bricht bene birneist bras
as silver wrocht at all devys,
and als gud drinking out of glas
as gold, thocht gold gif grittar prys.

The effect of the following stanza (from 'How
suld my febill body fure' [100]) is partly to degrade the
situation:

For nobillis hes nocht ay renown,
nor gentillis ay the gayest gown.
Thay cary victuallis to the town
    that werst dois dine.
Sa bissely to busk I boun,
ane uthir eitis the berry doun
    that suld be mine.

The images are rustic and appetitive. At the same
time, they intrude into a courtly poem something
of the reality of poverty and injustice as experienced
by a peasant sensibility. In addition, the first two
lines hint that while Scott suffers like a peasant, he
retains the courtier's finer sensitivities. Such complexity, to say the least, is unusual in the poetry of
courtly love.

Scott was also an accomplished performer in the
high style, which most modern tastes find less
congenial than the middle and low. It is probably

fair to say that for twentieth-century readers his greatest achievement is to combine the singing with the speaking voice in poems which after four centuries still preserve their urgency and flavour.

IN ALL ITS PHASES, Scott's poetry seems to attract and influence his contemporaries. I have more than once mentioned the possibility of a relationship to Wyatt. Several of the best anonymous poems in this collection parallel or echo Scott's style and phraseology. One might particularly single out 'My hairt is heich above', 'In to the nycht' and 'So prayis me as ye think caus quhy'.[101] It would seem reasonable to assume that all those poems were written between 1540 and 1560.

Alexander Montgomerie, as the reader may recollect,[102] links Scott as a poet with Robert Semple—a link which would not readily come to mind if one were to judge in terms only of the certain surviving work of either poet. Dempster, however, attributes to Semple a collection of love poems, *carmina amatoria*,[103] the existence of which is doubted or denied by the few scholars who have considered the matter. Even if they actually existed, it is certain that none has survived with a direct attribution to Semple. In his political poems, however, many of which were necessarily published anonymously or pseudonymously, Semple had the habit of including at some point a punning reference to his own name, a reference which would indicate the authorship to members of his own circle without bringing him much general public attention. In 'The Regent's Tragedie', for instance, one finds:[104]

> This fair ye weill: I flait not to offend you
> in sempill veirs this Schedull that I send you.

In 'Maddeis Proclamatioun' he writes (in the adopted person of a market-woman):

> For I, a wife with sempill life,
> dois win my meit ilk day,
> for small availl, ay selling caill,
> the best fassoun I may,

and in 'The Spur to the Lordis':

> This Rakles Robert did report
> in raggit Ruffyis ryme;
> sen Sempill solace to this sort
> availlis maist in this time.

Those are only a few of several instances which might be quoted.

The same punning habit recurs, or seems to recur in two anonymous lyrics, 'Quhen I think on my lady deir' and 'The well of vertew and flour of woman-hede'.[105] The first contains a single, but convincing, instance, the couplet

> Thocht scho be cumd of grit degre,
> and thou be cumin of sempill kin,

which closely parallels some of the certain instances from the political poems. The second is more complex. The pun is as convincing:

> to your magnificens
> I me commend, as I haif done befoir,
> my sempill hairt for now and evir moir.

The poem, moreover, was almost certainly addressed to a woman called Grisel (Grizelda), as is shown by the reference to the heroine of Chaucer's *Clerk's Tale* in the second and third lines:

> patrone unto patiens,
> lady of lawty bayth in word and deid.

The final stanza lays much emphasis on the nobility of the name borne by the lady: it is 'gentle', a word opposed to 'sempill' in a way which suggests something more than a surface opposition:

> Ye beir the name of gentilnes of blud,
> ye beir the name that mony for you deis,
> ye beir the name ye ar bayth fair and gud,
> ye beir the name that faris than you seis,
> ye beir the name fortoun and ye aggreis,
> ye beir the name of landis of lenth and breid,
> the well of vertew and flour of womanheid.

All those peculiarities, I suggest, come into focus if one supposes that the poem was addressed by Robert Semple, a man of no particular social consequence, to Lady Grisel Semple, daughter of Robert, third Lord Semple, one of the major Catholic magnates in the Scotland of the time. It makes little difference—and may even add to the poignancy of the poem—that Lady Grisel's real qualities were almost the reverse of those attributed to her in the poem.[106] She was the second wife of James Hamilton of Stenhouse, Captain of Edinburgh Castle, and afterwards Provost of that city. He was killed in 1548, two years after he had divorced Lady Grisel. By 1545 she had become the mistress of his kinsman, the Governor Arran's bastard half-brother John Hamilton, Abbot of Paisley, who in 1549 became Archbishop of St Andrews in succession to the murdered Cardinal Beaton. It was largely at Hamilton's instigation that Arran as governor adopted the policies which included major reliance on the French alliance, confirmed in 1548 by the Treaty of Haddington, which sent the young Queen Mary to France, and in 1549 brought Arran the French dukedom of Châtelherault. Hamilton's liaison with Lady Grisel lasted for many years, and was a major cause of scandal to the protestant party. Hamilton was hanged in 1571 for his alleged complicity in the murder of the Regent Moray. Lady Grisel died in 1575.

Nor is this all. 'Quhen I think on my lady deir' contains an apparent adaptation of a verse from Scott's 'Luve preysis but comparesone':

Oft time hes bene hard and sene
ane loird hes luvit ane las full weill,
and eik a laid ane lady scheyne,
so Luf of Fortoun turnis hir quheill.

In turn, Scott's poem may be more complicated than at first appears. It contains the same apparent pun on the name Semple, again linked suggestively to the word 'gentle':

Luve preysis but comparesone
both gentill, sempill, generall

The pun recurs somewhat later in the poem:

So service cumis of sympilnes.

Of itself, the parallel might seem unimportant, were

it not for the fact that the poem seems also in many ways to refer to the situation sketched in the previous paragraph. In the first stanza, for instance, the lines which are separated only by a couplet from the gentill/sempill opposition,

> For luve makis nobill ladeis thrall
> to bassir men of birth and blud,

might easily be taken as a reference to the liaison between John Hamilton and Lady Grisel Semple, not least in terms of the reference to the baser blood of the male partner. So later a double meaning is perhaps to be seen in the lines:

> Scho suld my service find als reddy
> as duke to duches docht him dres.
> For as proud princely luve expres
> is to haif soverenitie

In 1549, the only duke in Scotland was Arran after his promotion to the French dukedom of Châtel-herault. Arran was also heir-presumptive to the Scottish throne, and had hopes either of himself becoming king, or at least of marrying his son to Queen Mary.[107]

It is difficult to see Scott's poem as primarily anything other than a satiric portrayal of the vagaries of love, but neither is it difficult to see that the portrait might have relevance to the political actualities of 1549 or 1550 in Scotland. Semple's verses in turn might either be genuine love poems addressed to Lady Grisel, or alternatively attempts, using her instrumentality, to win favour with the Governor and the Archbishop.

Bannatyne includes in his anthology two lyrics[108] by Alexander Montgomerie (1545–1597) who in the 1580s was to become the master poet at the court of the young James VI. Montgomerie, in turn, links the pre-Reformation Scottish lyric to such post-Reformation developments as the sonnet. For the most part, however, the old culture withered, and after 1568 its disappearance is emblematized by the tranformation of Robert Semple to a verse-pamphleteer and by the silence, for whatever cause, of Alexander Scott.

The courtly love lyric in Scottish Gaelic

Although connections and interrelations have never been established in detail, Scottish Gaelic court poetry of the fifteenth century has some relevance (even simply as a parallel) for the development of the courtly love lyric in Middle Scots. The actual existence of parallels between the traditions is obvious—for instance, the MS *Book of the Dean of Lismore*[109] is in many ways a Gaelic equivalent to the collections of Bannatyne and Maitland. It was compiled between 1512 and 1526 by sir James Mac-Gregor, Dean of Lismore in Argyll and vicar of Fortingall in Perthshire. He was assisted, probably among others, by his brother, the poet Donnchadh mac Dubhghaill Mhaoil. The Scottish poems in the collection belong for the most part to the middle and late fifteenth and early sixteenth centuries, and the great majority are court poems, composed, not for the royal court, but for those of the major Highland chiefs, notably the houses owing allegiance to the MacDonalds, Lords of the Isles, to the Earls of

Argyll, and to the chiefs of Clan Gregor (the clan to which the compiler and his brother belonged). Panegyric, lament and satire are the dominant modes, and there are many references to contemporary events.

Much of this, it is obvious, has no connection with lyric poetry of the type we are discussing. The poetry, nevertheless, is court poetry, and the courts for which the Gaelic bards composed were by no means entirely divorced from the manners and customs of the royal and noble courts of the Lowlands. *Amour courtois*, in particular, had become a subject for bardic composition more than two centuries before the Dean of Lismore compiled his anthology.[110] Most of the surviving courtly love lyrics are of Irish rather than Scottish Gaelic provenance, but it is notable that the Dean preserves two from Scottish courts of the middle fifteenth century.

Those lyrics form an appendix to this collection. They are attributed to Iseabal Ní Mheic Cailéin, Isabel, that is most probably to say, wife of Colin, first Earl of Argyll (1457–93).

1 *The Maitland Folio Manuscript* edited by W. A. Craigie for the Scottish Text Society (2 vols., Edinburgh and London 1919, 1927). The quotation is from 'Satire on the Age', I, 37–40. The MS was in course of compilation between *c.* 1570 and Maitland's death in 1586.

2 See W. Tod Ritchie *The Bannatyne Manuscript* (*STS*, 4 vols., Edinburgh and London 1928–34). The majority of the poems in this collection are taken from the fourth part of Bannatyne's anthology, a part which he himself entitled 'Ballattis of Luve'. The anthology was completed during the months of plague which afflicted Edinburgh in 1568.

3 Edinburgh University MS La. III. 483, pp. 176–7. See also H. S. P. Hutchison *The St Andrews Psalter* (unpublished Edinburgh University Mus. D. dissertation, 1957).

4 See R. L. Mackie *King James IV of Scotland* (Edinburgh and London 1958), especially chapter V, 'Scotland in 1503'; J. Durkan 'Education in the Century of the Reformation', 'The Cultural Background in Sixteenth-Century Scotland', both in D. McRoberts (ed.) *Essays on the Scottish Reformation* (Glasgow 1962).

5 H. Harvey Wood *The Poems and Fables of Robert Henryson* (2nd ed., Edinburgh and London 1958) p. 136; J. MacQueen *Robert Henryson* (Oxford 1967) pp. 38–43. See also below pp. xvi–xvii.

6 'Remonstrance to the King', W. Mackay Mackenzie *The Poems of William Dunbar* (2nd ed. revised by Bruce Dickins, London 1960) p. 36.

7 'The Palice of Honour' 490–528; Priscilla J. Bawcutt *The Shorter Poems of Gavin Douglas* (*STS*, Edinburgh and London 1967) pp. 38–41.

8 Nos. XVII and XVIII of the present collection. Bawcutt, pp. 44–7, 68–9.

9 Edited by J. A. H. Murray (*EETS. ES*, XVII–XVIII, London 1872–3).

10 Edited by A. F. Mitchell (*STS*, Edinburgh and London 1897).

11 See especially K. Elliott and H. M. Shire *Musica Britannica*, XV, 'Music of Scotland' (London 1957): P. M. Young *A History of British Music* (London 1967) pp. 111–15.

12 Most conveniently consulted in J. Kinsley *Ane Satyre of the Thrie Estaitis* (London 1954). The first song referred to occurs

at line 326; the second at line 1025. See also J. MacQueen 'Ane Satyre of the Thrie Estaitis', *Studies in Scottish Literature*, III (January 1966) 129–43.

13 Edited by J. Kinsley (London and Edinburgh 1959).

14 Nos. III and IV of the present collection. The text is taken from the edition of W. Mackay Mackenzie (London 1939). For the probable date of the poem, see J. MacQueen 'Tradition and the Interpretation of the *Kingis Quair*', *R.E.S.*, n.s. XII (1961) pp. 117 ff.

15 F. N. Robinson *The Works of Geoffrey Chaucer* (2nd ed., Boston and London 1957) p. 815.

16 See especially H. A. Mason *Humanism and Poetry in the Early Tudor Period* (London 1958) pp. 165 ff.; J. Stevens *Music and Poetry in the Early Tudor Court* (London 1961), chapter 10, 'The Courtly Makers from Chaucer to Wyatt'; R. Southall *The Courtly Maker* (Oxford 1964), chapter III, '"Troilus and Criseyde": A Point of Departure'.

17 No. II of the present collection. *The Temple of Glas* is most conveniently consulted in J. Norton-Smith *John Lydgate. Poems* (Oxford 1966) pp. 67–112. It is worth noting that Bannatyne also includes a version of *The Letter of Cupid* (1402) by Thomas Hoccleve (*c.* 1368–*c.* 1437), as no. CCCLXI of his collection (Tod Ritchie, IV, pp. 49–63). His attribution of the poem to Chaucer perhaps shows that he was working from Thynne's 1532 edition of Chaucer, which includes this poem.

18 Robinson, p. 490.

19 892. Norton-Smith, p. 94.

20 Minerva.

21 Mackay Mackenzie, pp. 104–7.

22 No. XLVII of the present collection. I suggest later in this introduction that the poem may be the work of the Protestant versifier, Robert Semple.

23 Mackay Mackenzie, pp. 20–3.

24 Tod Ritchie, IV, 48–9.

25 Tod Ritchie, IV, 13–14: The majority of Dunbar's own love-poems markedly resemble those of Mersar and Clerk.

26 Edited by R. L. Graeme Ritchie (4 vols., *STS*, Edinburgh and London 1925–9).

27 Graeme Ritchie II, 107.

28 No. V of the present collection.

29 Edited by M.M.Gray for the Scottish Text Society (Edinburgh and London 1912).

30 See especially *Music and Poetry*, chapter 10, *The Courtly Maker*, chapter IV.

31 See especially B.Vogel 'Secular Politics and the Date of *Lancelot of the Laik*', *Studies in Philology*, xl (1943) 4–5.

32 E.G.Cody and W.Murison *The Historie of Scotland*, II (*STS* Edinburgh and London 1895) p. 97 and footnote.

33 Oxford, 1952.

34 No. VI of the present collection.

35 Nos. XVII and XVIII of the present collection. See also above footnote 7.

36 p. 286.

37 Nos. VIII and X of the present collection.

38 No. XXII of the present collection.

39 Robbins, p. 150.

40 Robbins, pp. 208–9.

41 *English Literature in the Sixteenth Century Excluding Drama* (Oxford 1954) pp. 99–100. The poem is no. XXIV of the present collection.

42 Hutchison, pp. 178–9.

43 *Accounts of the Lord High Treasurer of Scotland*, VIII, 1541–1546, p. 54.

44 *Registrum Secreti Sigilli*, 1542–1548, no. 1026, 12 January 1544/45.

45 *Extracts from the Council Register of the Burgh of Aberdeen*, 1398–1570 (Spalding Club, Aberdeen 1844) p. 207 (18 September 1544).

46 Ibid. pp. 239–40.

47 *Registrum Secreti Sigilli*, 1567–1574, no. 487, 13 September 1568.

48 Scottish Record Office, *Register of Deeds*, I, f.317v.

49 Robert Pitcairn (ed.) *Criminal Trials and Other Proceedings before the High Court of Justiciary in Scotland*, Part X, M.D. XXXVII–M.D. LXVIII (Bannatyne Club 1833) p. 400.

50 *Register of Deeds* III, f.129v.

51 Scottish Record Office, *Books of Assumption*, E.48 I/1, f.259.

52 *Register of Deeds*, VI, f. 155.

53 See, for instance, *Register of Deeds*, VIII, f.321 (15 May 1566).

54 *Register of Deeds*, VII, f.318v.

55 No. XXVII of the present collection.

56 For biographical details, see the index entry in W.Croft Dickinson *John Knox's History of the Reformation in Scotland* (2 vols., London and Edinburgh 1949), and the MS *Fasti Ecclesiae Scoticanae Medii Aevi* in the Scottish Record Office.

57 Croft Dickinson, I, p. 19.

58 G.Donaldson 'The Parish Clergy and the Reformation', *Essays on the Scottish Reformation*, p. 142.

59 Croft Dickinson, op. cit., I. 29. The details in this paragraph are derived from D.Hamer *The Works of Sir David Lindsay of the Mount* (4 vols., STS, Edinburgh and London 1931–6) III, 113. 'The Complaint . . . of Bagsche' will be found in I, 92–9.

60 'Some Aspects of the Early Renaissance in Scotland', *Forum for Modern Language Studies*, III, 3 (July 1967) 219–20. See also the appendix to my Warton Lecture, 'Alexander Scott and Scottish Court Poetry of the Middle Sixteenth Century' (Oxford 1969). The poem is no. XXXV of the present collection.

61 M. Connat 'Documents Inédits du Minutier Central', *Bibliothèque d'Humanisme et Renaissance*, XII (1950) p. 113. I owe this reference to Dr John Durkan.

62 Ed. P. Harvey and J. E. Heseltine (Oxford 1959).

63 *Registrum Secreti Sigilli*, 1529–1542, no. 2899, 28 February 1538/39. See also *Accounts of the Lord High Treasurer of Scotland*, 1473–1498, p. ccxxxiv and footnote 3; p. 67.

64 No. XXXVI of the present collection.

65 J. R. N. Macphail *Papers from the Collection of Sir William Fraser* (Scottish History Society, Edinburgh 1924) pp. 223–4.

66 'Education in the Century of the Reformation', D. Mc-Roberts (ed.) *Essays on the Scottish Reformation* (Glasgow 1962) p. 149 and footnote.

67 *Registrum Secreti Sigilli*, 1542–1548, no. 2876. The place of issue was the abbey of Haddington. The town was then occupied by the English and besieged by a joint Franco-Scottish force. The treaty by which the Scots agreed to Mary's French marriage was signed at Haddington on 7 July 1548.

68 No. 2877, same place and date.

69 G. Donaldson *Accounts of the Collectors of Thirds of Benefices* (Scottish History Society, Edinburgh 1949) pp. 86–7.

70 J. Cranstoun *The Poems of Alexander Scott* (STS, Edinburgh and London 1896) pp. 23–5.

71 Cranstoun, pp. 1–8.

72 *Registrum Magni Sigilli*, 1546–1580, no. 395.

73 No. XLII of the present collection.

74 *Registrum Secreti Sigilli*, 1556–1567, no. 3213.

75 W. A. Lindsay, J. Dowden and J. Maitland Thomson *Charters, Bulls and Other Documents relating to the Abbey of Inchaffray (SHS,* Edinburgh 1908) p. 168; Scottish Record Office *Calendar of Charters and other original Documents,* IX (AD 1560–1567) no. 1944.

76 *Register of Deeds,* IX, f.217.

77 *Register of Deeds,* XI, f.238.

78 *Register of Deeds,* XVIII, f.153. This document is much damaged by damp.

79 *Register of Deeds,* XX, f.442 v. This document is torn and much damaged by damp.

80 *Register of Deeds,* XXI, f.250 v.

81 Cranstoun, p. 101.

82 CLXXXV–CXCI; Tod Ritchie II, pp. 325–49.

83 *Register of Deeds,* XXIII, ff.59 v., 68 v. For further biographical details, see A. J. Mill *Mediaeval Plays in Scotland* (Edinburgh and London 1927) p. 199 and footnote 3.

84 No. XXX of the present collection.

85 No. XXXI of the present collection.

86 No. XXXII of the present collection.

87 No. XXXIII of the present collection

88 No. XXXIV of the present collection.

89 No. XXXVII of the present collection.

90 No XXIX of the present collection.

91 No. XXXVIII of the present collection.

92 Nos. XXXIX and XL of the present collection.

93 Cranstoun, p. 192. Whenever music has been preserved for a poem by Scott, one must consider the possibility that Scott also wrote the tune.

94 No. XLII of the present collection. Notice Bannatyne's colophon, quoted above, p. *xli.*

95 No. XLIV of the present collection.

96 No. XLIII of the present collection.

97 No. XLVI of the present collection.

98 No. XLV of the present collection.

99 'Of May', 46–50; Cranstoun, p. 24.

100 No. XLI of the present collection. A tune has survived for this poem. (Cranstoun, pp. 185–6).

101 Nos. L, LI and LII of the present collection.

102 Above, pp. *xliv–xlv*.

103 *Historia Ecclesiastica Gentis Scotorum* (Bannatyne Club, Edinburgh 1829) p. 602. '*Scripsit . . . carmina amatoria, ut Propertii sanguinem, Tibulli lac, Ovidii mel, Callimachi sudorem, equasse plerisque doctis videatur, Lib. I.*'

104 J. Cranstoun *Satirical Poems of the Time of the Reformation* (Scottish Text Society, 2 vols., Edinburgh and London 1891). The quotations will be found in vol. I, pp. 105, 149, 159. Compare, too, Brother Kenneth 'The Popular Literature of the Scottish Reformation', *Essays on the Scottish Reformation*, pp. 169–84.

105 Nos. XLVII and XLVIII of the present collection.

106 Croft Dickinson *Knox's History*, i, 59; ii. 485–6.

107 W. Croft Dickinson *Scotland from the Earliest Times to 1603* (London and Edinburgh 1961) pp. 261–4; G. Donaldson *Scotland. James V – James VII* (Edinburgh and London 1965) p. 66.

108 Nos. LVI and LVII of the present collection.

109 *Scottish Verse from the Book of the Dean of Lismore*, edited by W. J. Watson (Scottish Gaelic Texts Society, Edinburgh 1937); *Heroic Poetry from the Book of the Dean of Lismore*, edited by Neil Ross (*SGTS*, Edinburgh 1939).

110 See 'Love's Bitter-Sweet', chapter VI in R. Flower, *The Irish Tradition* (Oxford 1947); T. F. O'Rahilly *Dánta Grádha* (Dublin and Cork 1926).

Although at first sight the spelling and some usages of fifteenth- and sixteenth-century Scots may seem strange and unsystematic, the variations are seldom arbitrary. Commonsense, together with a knowledge of a few rules and relationships, will greatly reduce the difficulty. These notes form a brief aid to reading which obviously and deliberately is not exhaustive. All examples are taken from the texts.

The sign = should be expanded as 'corresponds etymologically to'. The meaning of the Scots and English words is not always identical.

Orthography, Phonology—Vowels
Three spelling conventions may sometimes cause difficulty.
(i) The combination *a/e/o/y* + *i* often indicates a long vowel, not a diphthong; *caild* = cold; *cleir* = clear; *hoip* = hope; *pryis* = prize.
(ii) In the combination *-al* + consonant, *-al-* represents a sound which in Modern Scots is often represented by *-au-*; *chalmer* = chamber; *haldis* = holds (Mn. Scots *hauds*); *Malkyn* = Maukyn; *walking* = waking (Mn. Scots *waukin*).
(iii) *quh-* corresponds to English *wh-*.
One other point may be added. *-is* is usually pronounced *-s*, but for metrical reasons it may be treated as a separate unstressed syllable. Compare the two pronunciations of *hairtis* in the following couplet:

> *Sen ye ar, hairt, with bayth our hairtis possesst,*
> *my hairt is in your hairtis governance.*

Phonology—Consonants
The most obvious difficulties are as follows:
(i) *c/k* may correspond to English *ch*: *kirk* = church; *sic* = such.
(ii) *-ch-* may correspond to English *-gh-*: *bricht* = bright; *heich* = high; *lachand* = laughing; *strecht* = straight.
(iii) Metathesis of *-r-* is not uncommon; *brynt* = burnt; *bryst* = burst; *thretty* = thirty.

Accidence
(i) In the noun, *-is*, *-ys* may be either a plural or a possessive ending (see the couplet quoted above).
(ii) In the present indicative active of the verb, where the subject is not the personal pronoun, or where the subject personal pronoun does not immediately precede the verb,

the ending of the 1st, 2nd and 3rd person, singular and plural, is *-is* or *-ys*. *-is* or *-ys* is the invariable ending of the 2nd and 3rd singular: *no moir I lowt, bot standis up stout: so neidis thou; we kiss and cossis hairts; my leivis lyis out.*

(iii) *-and* is the ending of the present participle; *flurisand* = flourishing; *joyand* = joying; *lachand* = laughing; *makand* = making; *standand* = standing.

(iv) *-in, -yn* are endings of the past participle in strong verbs: *bundin* = bound; *cumin* = come; *fundin* = found.

(v) *-t, -it, -yt* are endings of the past participle in weak verbs: *commandit* = commanded; *fulfillit* = fulfilled; *polist* = polished.

In this edition I have expanded abbreviations, treated *ff* as *F* or *f*, and *fs* as *s*, normalized the use of *þ; ȝ; u, v* and *w; i, j* and *y*. MS. capitals, other than those which correspond to modern usage, have been removed. Where *the* or *þe* represents 'thee' or where *to* represents 'too', I have expanded to *thee* or *too*. Punctuation is editorial and obvious mistakes have been silently emended. Where the spelling *evill* clearly represents the word *ill*, I have so emended it. Capitalization is editorial.

Air and lait, early and late
als, as
and, and, if
ane, a, an, one

Bene, am, is, are
bot, but, without
bot gif, save if
brukle, frail
but, without, save for

Cors, body

De, die
dede, deid, often 'death' rather than 'dead' or 'deed'
dre, endure

Ene, eyes
erd, earth

Fra, fro, from

Gang, go
gar, cause
gif(e), if, give

He, heich, high
hing, hang
hir, her
howp, hope
hyne, hence

Ilk, each

Ken, know

Laif, lave, rest, remainder
laill, leill, loyal, faithful
lawty, loyalty, faithfulness
levys, lives

Ma, mo, more
mais, makes
maist, moist, most
man, mon, must
may, maid, maiden, girl
meikle, much
mene, complain
mot, may

Nane, none
nocht, not, nothing
nor, than

Ocht, anything
oft sys, often
ony, any
or, ere, before

Quhilk, which
quhill, while, until
quhone, when

Rin, ryn, run

Sa, so
salbe, shall be, will be
sall, shall
scedull, sedull, letter, poem
schene, bright, beautiful
schent, ruined, destroyed
scho, she
sen, since
sic, such
sich, sigh
sone, soon
spreit, sprete, spirit, courage
syne, then, afterwards

Than, then
thir, these

this, this, thus
thocht, though, although
thoill, endure, bear
throucht, *throw*, *thrucht*,
   through
til(l), to
tyne, lose

Wait, know, knows
walk, wake, waken
weill, well
went, wend, go
weycht, *wicht*, man, person
without, unless, without
wyt, blame

Yeid, went

BALLATTIS OF
LUVE

*

GEOFFREY CHAUCER *c*.1343–1400

I

The song of Troyalus

1

GIFE no luve is, o God quhat feill I so?
And gif luve is, quhat thing and quhiche is he?
Gife luve be gud, frome quhence cummys my wo?
Gife it be wicke, a wondir thinketh me
quhan every turment and adversite
that cummeth of him, may to me savery think;
for ay thrust I the more that iche it drink.

2

And gif that at mine awin lust I brenne,
frome whence cummys my waling and my playnt?
Gife harme agree me, quhairto plene I thane?
I not, ne quhy unwery that I faint.
O quick deth! O sweit harme so queynt!
How may of thee in me be suche quantete,
bot gif that I consent that it so be?

3

And gif I consent, I wrongfully
complene, ywis. Thus possed to and fro
all steirles within a bot am I

---

thrust, thirst. *iche*, I. *brenne*, burn. *I not*, I do not know.
quick, living. *queynt*, strange. *possed*, pushed, tossed.
steirles, without a rudder. *bot*, boat.

3

amid the se, atwixin wondis two
that incontrair standen ever mo.
Allas! quhat is this wondir maledye?
For heit of cold, for cold of heit I die.

4

And to the God of Luve thus said he
with pitous voce, 'O lord, now youris is
my spreit, quhiche that aucht youris be.
You thank I, lord, that haif me brocht to this.
Bot quhither goddes or woman ywis
scho be, I not wiche, that ye do me serve,
bot as hir man I wolle ay leve and sterve.

5

Ye standyn in hir ene mychtely,
as in a place to your vertew digne;
quhairfoir, lord, gife my service or I
may lykin you to be to me benigne.
For my estait royell heir I resigne
in to hir hand, and with hummill cheir
becoim hir man, as to my lady deir.'

Quod Chauseir of Troyelus

wondis, winds. _mo_, more. _aucht_, ought. _ene_, eyes.
digne, worthy, suitable.

Bannatyne CCLXXXIII, f.230a-b; Chaucer _Troilus and
Criseyde_ I, 400–34. See Introduction, pp. xvii–xviii. There are
some interesting textual variants.

2.2. whence, MS _whench_. 2.3. agree, MS _agreve_. 4.2. now,
MS _no_.

II

1

IN TO my hairt emprentit is so soir
hir schap, hir forme and eik hir seymlines,
hir port, hir cheir, hir gudnas mair and mair,
hir womanheid and eik hir gentilnes,
hir trewth, hir faith and also hir meiknes,
with all verteous, iche set in his degre;
thair is no lak bot onlie off pete.

2

Hir sad demenyng, of will nocht variable,
off louke benyng and rut of all plesans,
and exampillair to all that bene stable,
discreit, prudent, of wisdome sufficiens,
mirrour of wit, grund of gud governans,
a warld of bewty compasit in hir face,
quhois persant luk did throcht my hart race.

3

Quhat wondir is than thocht I be with dreid
inly supprysit for to askin grace
of hir that is a quene of womanheid?

---

verteous, virtues. *iche*, each. *persant*, piercing.
throcht, through. *supprysit*, overpowered.

5

For weill I wat that in so he a place
I will nocht be in dispair in no caice,
bot suffir lawly thus that I indure,
till scho of pietie tak me in hir cure.

---

he, high.

Bannatyne C C L V I I, f.220b; Lydgate *The Temple of Glas*, 743–56, 764–70. See Introduction, p. xviii.

2.1. demenyng, M S *demyng*, Lydgate *demening*.
2.7. persant, M S *present*, Lydgate *persant*; race, M S *glace*, Lydgate *race*. 3.2. supprysit, M S *suppoysit*, Lydgate *supprised*.
3.5–7. Lydgate, I wil not ben; therfor I overpace
And take louli what wo that I endure Til she of pite me take unto hir cure.

Songs from *The Kingis Quair*

III

O VENUS clere, of goddis stellifyit,
to quhom I yelde homage and sacrifis,
fro this day forth your grace be magnifyit,
that me ressavit have in suich wise
to lyve under your law and do servis;
now help me furth, and for your merci lede
my hert to rest, that deis nere for drede.

IV

QUHEN sall your merci rew upon your man,
quhois service is yit uncouth unto you?
Sen, quhen ye go, ther is noght ellis than:
bot, hert! quhere as the body may noght throu,
folow thy hevin! quho suld be glad bot thou
that suich a gyde to folow has undertake?
Were it throu hell, the way thou noght forsake!

---

stellifyit, made a star (? planetary). *uncouth*, unknown.
than, then. *throu*, through. *quhere as the body may noght throu*,
although the body can not escape to join you there.

MS Selden B.24 (Bodleian Library); *The Kingis Quair*,
ed. by W. Mackay Mackenzie (London 1939) stanzas
52 and 63. See Introduction, pp. xvii–xx.

V

from *The Buik of Alexander*, 1438

QUHEN I se hir forrow me,
that is fulfillit of all bounte,
and I behald hir colour cleir,
hir hare, that to fine gold is feir,
hir cheke, hir chin, hir middle small,
hir fare-hede and her fassoun all,
I am sa movit throw that sicht
that I have nouther strenth nor micht
to heir, to se, na yit to fele.
As man suld de, this wait I wele,
thus am I staid before that fre,
for hir that all my lufe suld be.

---

forrow, in front of. *feir*, equal. *fare-hede*, beauty.
staid, placed.

The Avowis of Alexander, printed by Alexander Arbuthnet,
Printer to the King's Majesty (Edinburgh *c.* 1580); *The
Buik of Alexander*, ed. by R. L. Græme Ritchie (4 vols., *STS*,
Edinburgh and London 1925–9) II, pp. 165–7, 2395–2406.

VI

Lancelot's soliloquy in prison

1

QUHAT have I gilt, allace! or quhat deservit.
that thus mine hart shal wondit ben and carvit
one by the sword of double peine and wo?
My comfort and my plesans is ago:
to me is nat that shuld me glaid reservit.

2

I curs the time of mine Nativitee,
Whar in the heven it ordinyd was for me
in all my lyve never til have ees,
but for to be example of dises:
and that apperith that every wicht may see.

3

Sen thelke time that I had sufficians
of age, and chargit thoghtis sufferans,
nor never I continewite haith o day
without the payne of thoghtis hard assay:
thus goith my youth in tempest and penans.

Quhat have I gilt, how have I been guilty? *carvit one*, carved
through. *ago*, gone. *glaid*, gladden. *thelke*, that same.
and chargit thoghtis sufferans, and (was) burdened with the
patient endurance of heavy thought. *nor never I continewite
haith o day*, I have never had a single continuous day.

4

And now my body is in presone broght;
but of my wo, that in regard is noght,
the wich mine hart felith ever more.
O deth, allace! why hath you me forbore
that of remed haith thee so long besoght!

---

bot of my wo, that in regard is noght, but that is nothing
in comparison with my woe.

MS KK. I. 5 (Cambridge University Library) ff.9b–10;
Lancelot of the Laik, ed. by M. M. Gray (*STS*, Edinburgh
and London 1912) 698–717. See Introduction, pp. xxiv–xxvii.

VII

1

ROBENE sat on gud grene hill
kepand a flok of fe:
mirry Makyne said him till,
'Robene, thou rew on me.
I haif thee lovit loud and still
thir yeiris two or thre:
my dule in dern bot gif thou dill,
dowtles but dreid I de.'

2

Robene anserit, 'Be the rude,
na thing of lufe I knaw,
but keipis my scheip undir yone wid—
lo! quhair thay raik on raw!
Quhat hes marrit thee in thy mude,
Makyne, to me thou schaw,
or quhat is lufe or to be lude:
fane wald I leir that law.'

3

'At luvis lair gife thou will leir,
tak thair ane *a b c*:

---

fe, sheep. *in dern*, secret, secretly. *dill*, assuage. *wid*, wood.
raik, go, wander. *lude*, loved. *leir*, learn.

11

be heynd, courtas and fair of feir,
wise, hardy and fre;
so that no denger do thee deir,
quhat dule in dern thou dre,
preis thee with pane at all poweir:
be patient and previe.'

4

Robene anserit hir agane,
'I wait nocht quhat is luve,
but I haif mervell in certane
quhat makis thee this wanrufe:
the weddir is fair and I am fane,
my scheip gois haill aboif:
and we wald play us in this plane,
thay wald us bayth reproif.'

5

'Robene, tak tent unto my taill
and wirk all as I reid
and thou sall haif my hairt all haill
eik and my madinheid:
sen God sendis bute for baill
and for murning remeid,
i dern with thee bot gif I daill,
dowtles I am bot deid.'

---

heynd, gracious, gentle. *feir*, bearing, demeanour. *deir*, harm,
hurt, injure. *dre*, bear, endure. *preis*, press, strive, contend.
this, thus. *wanrufe*, unhappy. *bute*, remedy.
i dern, secret, secretly. *daill*, have to do, deal.

6

'Makyne, to morne this ilk a tide
and ye will meit me heir,
peraventure my scheip ma gang besyd
quhill we haif liggit full neir:
bot maugre haif I and I byd
fra thay begin to steir:
quhat lyis on hairt I will nocht hyd:
Makyn, than mak gud cheir.'

7

'Robene, thou reivis me roif and rest:
I luve but thee allone.'
'Makyne, adew, the sone gois west,
the day is neir hand gone.'
'Robene, in dule I am so drest
that lufe wilbe my bone.'
'Ga lufe, Makyne, quhair evir thou list,
for lemman I lid none.'

8

'Robene, I stand in sic a styll,
I sicht and that full sair.'
'Makyne, I haif bene heir this quhyle:
at hame God gif I wair.'
'My huny Robene, talk ane quhill,
gif thou will do no mair.'
'Makyne, sum uther man begyle,
for hamewart I will fair.'

---

to morne, tomorrow. *liggit*, lain. *maugre haif I*, the devil take me.
byd, stay, remain. *steir*, move, stir. *reivis*, rob (of). *bone*, death.
lid, ? have loved. *styll*, plight.

9

Robene on his wayis went
als licht as leif of tre.
Mawkin murnit in hir intent
and trowd him nevir to se.
Robene brayd attour the bent.
Than Mawkyne cryit on hie,
'Now ma thou sing, for I am schent.
"Quhat alis lufe at me?"'

10

Mawkyne went hame withowttin faill,
full wery eftir cowth weip:
than Robene in a ful fair daill
assemblit all his scheip:
be that sum pairte of Mawkynis aill
outthrow his hairt cowd creip:
he fallowit hir fast thair till assaill
and till hir tuke gude keip.

11

'Abyd, abyd, thou fair Makyne,
a word for ony thing,
for all my luve it salbe thine
withowttin depairting:
all haill thy harte for till haif mine
is all my cuvating:
my scheip to morne quhill houris nine
will neid of no keping.'

---

brayd, moved quickly. *attour*, across. *bent*, field.
quhat alis lufe at me? What has love against me?

12

'Robene, thou hes hard soung and say
in gestis and storeis auld,
"The man that will nocht quhen he may
sall haif nocht quhen he wald."
I pray to Jesu every day
mot eik thair cairis cauld
that first presis with thee to play
be firth, forrest or fawld.'

13

'Makyne, the nicht is soft and dry,
the wedder is warme and fair,
and the grene woid rycht neir us by
to walk attour all quhair:
thair ma na janglour us espy
that is to lufe contrair:
thairin, Makyne, bath ye and I
unsene we ma repair.'

14

'Robene, that warld is all away
and quyt brocht till ane end,
and never agane thairto perfay
sall it be as thou wend,
for of my pane thou maid it play
and all in vane I spend.
As thou hes done, sa sall I say.
Murne on. I think to mend.'

---

gestis, tales. *eik*, increase. *firth*, wood, forest.
all quhair, everywhere. *janglour*, tell-tale.

15

HENRYSON

15

'Mawkyne, the howp of all my heill,
my hairt on thee is sett
and evirmair to thee be leill
quhill I may leif, but lett,
nevir to faill as utheris feill,
quhat grace that evir I gett.'
'Robene, with thee I will nocht deill.
Adew! for thus we mett.'

16

Malkyne went hame blyth annewche
attour the holttis hair:
Robene murnit and Malkyne lewche:
scho sang, he sichit sair,
and so left him bayth wo and wrewche
in dolour and in cair
kepand his hird under a huche
amangis the holtis hair.

---

heill, health, salvation. *leill*, faithful. *feill*, fail.
annewche, enough. *holttis*, woods.
hair, grey (*holttis hair* is a conventional rhyming tag).
lewche, laughed. *wrewche*, wretched. *huche*, crag.

Bannatyne CCCCII, ff.365a–366b. The poem does not have
a place in Bannatyne's Part IV, but any anthology of
fifteenth- and sixteenth-century Scottish love poems
would be incomplete without it.

16

VIII

1

FRESCHE fragrent flour of bewty soverane,
my hummill service tak nocht in disdane,
but me accep to be your serviture,
that in your cur with cair cotidiane
my spreit as thrall is fetterit to remane
that but your grace my life may nocht indure.
Your sycht hes slane my cors without recure.
But your remeid my lawbour is in vane
that luvis you best abuve all creature.

2

And evir sall withouttin fenyeing,
to quhome my hairt I send in governyng,
wondit with dreid, abiding the confort
of you, my luf, maist bowsum and benyng,
quhois cristall ene unto my mind rolling
revellis my pane but solace or repoirt.
Ressaif to grace your servand, I exhort,
for, and ye list to mak me conforting,
all my diseis war turnit in dispoirt.

3

Moir amorus wes nevir erdlie wicht
be Natur wrocht of plesand bewty bricht,
quhome to behald ane hevin is of delyt,

---

bowsum, pleasant, agreeable, handsome.

17

of womanheid the mirrour schynand lycht,
quhilk is the rute of my remembrance rycht,
joyand my spreit the verteus to indyt
of you, lady, the spectakle perfyte
of all this warld apperand to my sycht.
I may nocht lest, your lufe and ye me nyt.

4

Go littill bill and be my advocat
onto my lady best modestiat;
bid hir haif rewth upoun hir luvar trew,
and mak hir hairt with mercy mytigat,
for in her lufe I am so laqueat
that I may nocht enchenge hir for no new.
I may forthink that evir I hir knew
to me in mind and scho be indurat,
all erdlie joy for evir moir adew!

5

Beseik that schene with hummill reverence
thee to resaif and haif remembrance
on me, hir servand, subject and hir thrall,
that of my wo scho haif compacience,
quhilk nevir did hir falt nor yit offence,
bot evir bowsum, obeyand to hir call
in word and deid hes bene and evir moir sall
with hairt and mind and all obeysance.
For thi for grace thou instantlie go call.

---

lest, remain alive. *nyt*, deny. *modestiat*, modest.
mytigat, grow milder. *laqueat*, ensnared.
forthink, repent. *bowsum*, obedient.
for thi, therefore.

6

Say also to that gudlie fair and fresche
of all my panis scho may me weill relesche
with breif in bill or bodwart send agane
quhilk mycht releif me of my havines.
My cors that, plungit dalie in distres,
upon hir grace sall evir moir remane
that merciles hir servand be nocht slane,
(quhilk and scho do, hir fame sall evir decres)
in hurt and hindering of hir gud name.

7

But wo wer me that it suld so betyd
that scho thairthrow be cald ane homicyd!
Thairfoir do grace and be nocht obstinat.
Without scho do, scho will be notifyd
a manslaar, and tharefoir ratefyd.
But O! allace! be nocht so indurat!
With mercy mak your malice mitigat!
I ask but grace quhilk nocht suld be denyd
for service done unto your hie estait.

8

Adew, fair weill, my lustre lady sweit!
Adew, my seill and confort of my spreit!
Als trew as steill I salbe to your grace.
Adew, my joy and paramour compleit!

---

relesche, release. *breif*, letter. *bill*, scroll. *bodwart*, message.
notifyd, proclaimed. *ratefyd*, confirmed. *lustre*, lustrous, brilliant.
seill, happiness, prosperity.

ANONYMOUS

My hairt with noy but gif ye just decreit
will me distroy throw amouris of your face.
Adew, my hairt, the flour of lustinece!
Quhen we depairt, with sorrow sone I meit,
with panis smart and sychis cald, allace!

---

noy, trouble. *bot gif ye just decreit,*
unless you decide precisely (or justly).

Bannatyne CCLV, ff219b–220a. See Introduction, p. xxvii.

5.9. For thi . . . call, MS *Go thi for grace thou instantlie call.*
6.5. My cors . . . upon, MS *My plungit cors that dalie in distres,
that on.*

20

ANONYMOUS

IX

from *Ma commendationis with humilitie*

1

LUF hes me wardit in ane park of pane:
with dolour is the dowbill dykis dicht,
and lust is foster with his bow and flane:
fro tre to tre he chaisis me in the nycht.
I weip, I wring; wes nevir ane weriar wicht.
Thus nycht and day with petous vox I cry:
wes nevir ane undir the sonis lycht
mair patient sufferrit proctory.

2

Wald ye send help sone with ane speid of hop,
and cast the dyk of dolour to the erd,
with lusty hairt than suld I gif ane loip,
and cum to you—I ken the gait onsperd.
My hairt is youris full steidfastlie unsteird,
fetterit full fast quhill ye mak it fre.
I send till you, most farrest in this erd,
ma commendationis with humilitie.

---

wardit, enclosed. *park*, enclosed land held by royal
grant or prescription for keeping beasts of the chase.
dykis, walls. *dicht*, finished off, decorated. *foster*, forester.
flane, arrow. *wring*, writhe. *proctory*, legal administration by
another. *speid*, assistance. *loip*, leap. *ken the gait onsperd*,
know the way without asking. *unsteird*, unchanged.
farrest, fairest.

Bannatyne CCLXIV, f.223b. First four stanzas omitted.

X

1

FAIR weill my hairt, fair weill bayth freind and
fair weill the weill of sweitast madicyne,
fair weill my lufe, bayth life and deth also,
fair weill blythnes, fairweill sweit lemmane mine,
fair weill the flour of colour gud and fine,
that fadis nocht for weddir wen nor weit,
no moir than in the somer sessone sweit.

2

How sall I do quhen I mon you forgo?
How sall I sing? How sall I glaid than be?
How sall I leif? I luve you and no mo
quhat sall I do? How sall I confort me?
How sall I than thir bittir panis dre
quhair now I haif als meikle as I may
of cairis cauld in syching everilk day.

3

Quhat sall I wryt in to this petous bill?
Quhat sall I say forowttin awdiens?

---

weill of sweitast madicyne, healing spring, medicinal well.
lemmane, lover, sweetheart. *wen,* black, gloomy. *leif,* live.
dre, endure. *forowttin awdiens,* without a hearing.

ANONYMOUS

Quhat sall I dyt for to declair my will?
Quhat sall I say as now to your presens?
I you beseik with all my diligens
throw your lustines and flour of womanheid
anis for me this bill to se and reid.

4

I can nocht say no moir in this prolong,
for I nocht wait gif it be profitable
for to declair you all my panis strong,
heir in to wret be word or be fabill,
or gif it be to you commendabill:
thairfoir as now this littill remembrance
ye tak and keip in to your governance.

---

dyt, compose, write. *anis*, once. *prolong*, prologue.

Bannatyne CCLXVII, f.225a. See Introduction, p. xxvii.

XI

1

In May in a morning I movit me one
throw a grene garding with gravis begone,
as leid without liking but langour allone
for misheis and murning makand my mone,
    but mo,
  with hairt als havy as a stone.
  Of covir confoirt had I none,
  as wy that wist of na wone,
    bot wandreth in wo.

2

For wo and wandreth I waik, I weip and I wring,
for on so mild without maik, that mais my
    murnyng.
Oft sys I syche for hir saik and sendill I sing.
Hir lillie lyre as the laik dois me langing
    for lufe.

---

me one, by myself, alone. *gravis*, groves. *with gravis begone*,
surrounded by trees. *leid*, person, man. *liking*, happiness.
misheis, misease, distress. *but mo*, without anything more,
and no more (a rhyming tag). *covir*, recovery.
confoirt, encouragement. *wy*, man. *wone*, dwelling.
wandreth, sorrow. *maik*, peer, equal. *mais*, makes. *oft sys*, often.
sendill, seldom. *lyre*, face, complexion. *laik*, fine bleached linen.

That brycht fra baill ma me bring
to kyth on me sum conforting,
wald scho bethink, that sweit thing,
    quhat panis I prufe.

3

Thocht pane but play be my pairt, I preis nocht
  to pleid,
sen I hir hecht all my hairt to steir and to leid,
to chyd as a cowart I call no remeid.
Sen scho wrocht wreth otwart, I wallow as the
  weid
    in weir.
  The fair that forgis this feid,
  may scho nocht sair rew that reid,
  gif scho gravis me to deid
    with doggit dangeir.

4

Sall dengeir thus with me deill? Is this hir
  decreit,
for lang service and leill, hir luvar forleit?

---

brycht, beautiful woman. *baill*, misery, suffering. *kyth*, show.
preis, press, attempt, try. *hecht*, promised, vowed.
sen scho wrocht wreth otwart, since she gave outward and visible
signs of displeasure (wrought wrath outward). *wallow*, grovel.
weid, weed, creeping plant. *in weir*, doubt, in fear. *feid*, feud.
reid, counsel, advice. *gravis me to deid*, drives me to an untimely
grave. *doggit*, crabbed, cruel. *dangeir*, disdain. *dengeir*, power to
command. *forleit*, forsake, abandon.

Scho is the hoip of my heill, alhaill I beheit
to fend with freindschipis feill, to fall at hir feit
      as thrall.
  Quhat evir scho wone, I wald weit.
  Fro I be gravit in greit,
  than hes scho servandis that ar sweit
      the fewar at call.

5

Thocht I wer reddy to graif, thinkis scho that
  ganand,
yit scho hes, and sall haif, my hairt in hir hand,
quhither scho schent or scho saif, I am hir
  servand
to leif hir leir our the laif quhill I am levand
      but les.
  I am so bunding in hir band,
  I wait no way to ganestand,
  but pray to that plesand
      of petie and pes.

6

Off pety and pes I hir pray, and plane I repent,
gif I haif wrocht ony way to wryth hir intent.

---

heill, physical wellbeing, health. *beheit*, promise. *fend*, defend.
feill, many. (*to fend with freindschipis feill*, to defend with many
acts of friendship). *wone*, (obscure). *weit*, (obscure). *fro I be grav*
in greit, after I am buried in earth. *ganand*, fit, suitable,
convenient. *schent*, harm. *leif*, trust. *leir*, lore, learning. *our*, ove
above. *the laif*, the rest, all others. *levand*, living. *les*, falsehood
bunding, bound. *band*, bond. *ganestand*, withstand, oppose.
pes, peace. *wryth*, distort.

Sen scho my murning meis may within a
    moment,
it war hir sin, I dar say, I suld thus be schent,
      saikles,
    Suld scho nocht dreid and dissent
    to martir me innocent,
    that fra hir will can nocht went
      for deid nor distres.

7

At hir will sall I wair my wit in this plit
to lufe hir wirschep weill mair than wantone
    delyt.
Will scho hir man than forfair, all wycht will
    hir wyt.
But scho cuvir me of cair, my confort is quyt
      for aye.
    Evir quhair scho will I wryt
    in hairtly plesans perfyt,
    to quhome direct I this dyt
      ane morning of May.

---

meis, appease. *saikles*, innocent. *went*, go, depart. *deid*, death.
wair, spend. *forfair*, destroy, bring to ruin. *all wycht*, every man.
wyt, blame, condemn. *cuvir me*, cause me to recover. *dyt*, poem.

Bannatyne CCLXIX, ff.225b–226a. The relatively archaic
alliterative style has induced me to place this poem and
no. XII so early in the collection. Notice in each the near
repetition of the opening words at the close, and the
concatenatio or linkage of stanzas by repetition, or variation
of key words from the final line of one stanza to the first
line of the next. Compare the similar but even more
elaborate alliterative stanzaic technique of *Pearl*. Compare,
too, the fifteenth-century Scottish alliterative romances.

XII

1

FLOUR of all fairheid, gif I sall found thee fra,
all gammis are me queid, so neir to grund I ga:
I may no mirthis ma: for sorrow my self I sla.
Thus wirkis scho me wa, that wlonkast is in
    weid,
that is bayth freind and fa and farest flour to feid.

2

So fair was nevir fygour; no fame on flud so
    quhyt:
so proper of portratour, sa pert no sa perfyt.
Hir lyre is lilly lyk, plesand forowttin plyt.
In bour is no so brycht beriall no blench flour
as is that hendly hycht menskyt with all honour.

---

fairheid, beauty. *found*, go travel. *thee fra*, from thee. *gammis*,
games, sport. *queid*, bad, evil. *ma*, make. *wlonkast*, fairest.
weid, dress. *feid*, nourish. *fame*, foam. *portratour*, figure.
pert, beautiful, pert. *plyt*, danger, risk, blame. *bour*, a lady's
private apartment. *beriall*, beryl. *blench flour*, white flower, lily
hendly, courteous. *hycht*, called, named. *menskyt*, adorned
(No beryl or white flower in a lady's apartment is as bright
as that courteous one, adorned with all honour, is known to be

3

I aw hir honour ay to serve hir bayth lait and air
with all the mirth I may, for now and evir mair,
the confort of my cair, the saifir of my sair;
quhair evir I found or fair, scho is formest in fay.
With hir I wald I wair durand quhill Domisday.

4

Thair wes nevir day that dew, nor dyamont
   sa deir,
na stane so haill of hew as is hir hyd and heir.
Hir ene as cristall cleir with luflie lawchand cheir,
his pawpis till perle ar peir, perfyt and
   poleist new.
And I may nych hir neir, than gon wer never
   my glew.

5

Unglaid I gloir as gleid, sen my gud luf was gone
for neir witles I weid. I luf bot hir allone
that hes my hairt, ichone als trew as turtill
   on stone.
I luf bot hir allone of all that levis on leid.
Thus lykis me my leman, the flour of all fairheid.

---

aw, owe. *saifir*, salver. *wair*, were. *durand*, remaining.
quhill, until. *dew*, dawned. *deir*, precious. *haill*, perfect.
hyd, skin, complexion. *heir*, hair. *lawchand*, laughing.
pawpis, breasts, paps. *nych*, approach, go near. *glew*, mirth, joy.
gloir, stare. *gleid*, ember. *weid*, fade away. *ichone*, each one.
on leid, among people, on earth.

Bannatyne CCLXXIII, f.227 a–b.

XIII

1

F A N E wald I luve, bot quhairabout?
Thair is so mony luvaris thairowt
that thair is left no place to me.
Quhairof I hovit now in dowt
gif I sowld luve or lat it be.

2

Sa mony ar thair ladeis treitis
with triumphand amowres balleitis,
and dois thair bewteis pryis so he,
that I find not bot daft consaitis
to say of luve. Bot lat it be.

3

Sum thinkis his lady lustiest:
sum haldis his lady for the best:
sum sayis his luve is *A per se*:
but sum forsuth ar so opprest
with luve, wer bettir lat it be.

4

Sum for his ladyis luve lyis seik,
suppois scho comptis it not a leik,
and sum drowpis doun as he wold die:

---

hovit, remained. *treitis*, entreat. *A per se*, a paragon.
seik, sick. *comptis*, regards, considers.

sum strykis doun a threid bair cheik
for luve, wer bettir lat it be.

5

Sum luvis lang and lyis behind:
sum luvis and freindschip can not find:
sum festnit is and ma not fle:
sum led is lyk the belly blind
with luve, wer bettir lat it be.

6

Thocht luve be grene in gud curage,
and be difficill till assuage,
the end of it is miserie.
Misgovernit youth makis gowsty age,
forbeir ye than, and lat it be.

7

But quha perfytly wald imprent,
sowld find his luve moist permanent:
luve God, thy prince, and freind, all thre:
treit weill thy self and stand content,
and latt all uthir luvaris be.

---

strykis doun a threid-bair cheik, stretches down a lean cheek,
i.e. grows thin and pale. *festnit*, fastened, tied.
belly blind, blind-folded person. *gowsty*, dismal, depressing.
Bot quha perfytly wald imprent, but he who would remain
perfectly and deeply fixed (in love).

CLERK

Bannatyne CCCXXXI, f.255a. See Introduction p. xxvii.
'Maister Johne Clerk' is one of the first poets to be
named by Dunbar in 'Lament for the Makaris':

> That scorpion fell hes done infek
> Maister Johne Clerk and James Afflek,
> Fra balat making and tragidie;
> *Timor mortis conturbat me.*
>   (57–60)

'Maister' implies that he was a university graduate.

6.5. than, MS *not*.

XIV

1

ALLACE, so sobir is the micht
of wemen for to mak debait
incontrair menis subtell slicht,
quhilk ar fulfillit with dissait.
With tressone so intoxicait
ar mennis mowthis at all ouris,
quhome in to trest no woman wait:
sic perrell lyis in paramouris.

2

Sum sweris that he luvis so weill
that he will de without remeid
bot gife that he hir freindschip feill,
that garris him sic langour leid,
and thocht he haif no dout of speid,
yit will he sich and schaw grit schouris
as he wald sterfe in to that steid:
sic perrell lyis in paramouris.

---

sobir, moderate. *incontrair*, against. *slicht*, sleight. *trest*, trust.
wait, knows. *speid*, success. *sterfe*, die. *steid*, place.

3

Athis to sweir and giftis to hecht
moir than he hes thretty fold,
and for hir honour for to fecht
quhill that his blude be cumin cold—
bot fra scho to his will is yold,
adew! fair weill thir somer flouris!
All grows in glas that semit gold:
sic perrell lyis in paramouris.

4

Than turnis he his saill annone
and passis to ane uthir port:
thocht scho be nevir so wobegone,
hir cairis cauld ar his confort.
Heirfoir I pray in termys schort,
Christ keip thir birdis bricht in bowris
fra fals luvaris and thair resort:
sic perrell lyis in paramouris.

---

athis, oaths, *hecht*, promise. *thretty*, thirty. *fecht*, fight.
birdis, ladies.

Bannatyne CCCLX, f.269a. Mersar also makes an
appearance in Dunbar's 'Lament'. See Introduction,
pp. xx–xxi.

3.5. Will is yold, MS *willis yold*.

XV

1

SWEIT rois of vertew and of gentilnes,
delytsum lyllie of everie lustynes,
richest in bontie and in bewtie cleir,
and everie vertew that is held most deir,
except onlie that ye ar mercyles.

2

In to your garthe this day I did persew:
thair saw I flowris that fresche wer of hew,
baithe quhyte and rid moist lusty wer to seyne,
and halsum herbis upone stalkis grene;
yit leif nor flour find could I nane of rew.

3

I dout that Merche, with his caild blastis keyne,
hes slane this gentill herbe that I of mene,
quhois petewous deithe dois to my hart sic pane
that I wald mak to plant his rute agane.
So confortand his levis unto me bene.

---

vertew, both (moral) virtue and medicinal property.
lustynes, delightfulness, loveliness. *garthe*, garden.
persew, proceed. *seyne*, see. *halsum*, wholesome, health-giving
(in a medical sense). *dout*, fear. *mene*, complain.
confortand, comforting, strengthening.

Maitland Folio CXLV. Notice the combined imagery of decorative garden flowers and medicinal herbs. The lady herself is the garden.

1.4. that is held most deir, MS *that is deir*. David Laing suggested the emendation (*The Poetical Works of William Dunbar*, 2 vols., Edinburgh 1834; Supplement, 1865).

XVI

Quhone he list to feyne

1

MY HARTIS tresure, and swete assured fo,
the finale endar of my life for ever;
the creuell brekar of my hart in two—
to go to deathe, this I deservit never:
o man slayar! quhill saule and life dissever
stint of your slauchtir. Allace! your man am I,
a thousand times that dois you mercy cry.

2

Have mercie, luif! have mercie, ladie bricht!
Quhat have I wrocht aganis your womanheid,
that ye suld murdir me, a sakles wicht,
trespassing never to you in word nor deid?
That ye consent thairto, O God forbid!
Leif creueltie, and saif your man for schame,
or throucht the warld quite losit is your name.

---

stint of, leave off, give up. *sakles*, innocent.

37

3

My deathe chasis my life so besalie
that wery is my goist to fle so fast;
sic deidlie dwawmes so mischeifaislie
ane hundrithe times hes my hairt ouirpast;
me think my spreit rynnis away full gast,
beseikand grace on kneis you befoir,
or that your man be lost for evermoir.

4

Behold my wod intollerabill pane,
for evermoir quhilk salbe my dampnage!
Quhy, undir traist, your man thus have ye slane?
Lo! deithe is in my breist with furious rage,
quhilk may no balme nor tryacle assuage,
bot your mercie, for laik of quhilk I de:
allace! quhair is your womanlie petie!

5

Behald my deidlie passioun dolorous!
Behald my hiddows hew and wo, allace!
Behald my mayne and murning mervalous,
withe sorrowful teris falling frome my face!
Rewthe, luif, is nocht, helpe ye not in this cace,
for how sould ony gentill hart indure
to se this sycht on ony creature!

---

dwawmes, fits of faintness. *gast*, terrified. *wod*, raging.
dampnage, damage, injury. *traist*, trust, *mayne*, moan.

6

Quhyte dow, quhair is your sobir humilnes?
Swete gentill turtour, quhair is your pete went?
Quhair is your rewthe? the frute of nobilnes,
off womanheid the tresour and the rent;
mercie is never put out of meik intent,
nor out of gentill hart is fundin petie,
sen mercyles may no weycht nobill be.

7

In to my mind I sall you mercye cry,
quhone that my toung sall faill me to speik,
and quhill that nature me my sycht deny,
and quhill my ene for pain incluse and steik,
and quhill the dethe my hart in sowndir breik,
and quhill my mind may think and towng may
    steir:
and syne, fair weill, my hartis ladie deir.

---

dow, dove. *turtour*, turtle-dove. *the tresour and the rent*,
the capital and the income. *incluse*, close. *steik*, shut. *steir*, stir.

Maitland Folio CXLVIII. The title is taken from the
colophon, 'Quod Dumbar quhone he list to feyne'. The
poem parodies the conventions and phraseology of the
courtly love lyric.

2.3. ye suld murdir, MS *ye murdir*. Laing suggested the
emendation.

XVII

A ballett of inconstant love

1

CONSTRENYT hart bylappit in distres,
groundit in wo and full of hevynes,
complene thy paynfull caris infinite.
Bewale this warldis frele unstedfastnes,
havand regrait, sen gone is thy glaidnes,
and all thy solace returnyt in dispyte.
O cative thrall, involupit in syte,
confesse thy fatale wofull wrechitnes,
divide in twane and furth diffound all tyte,
aggrevance gret in miserabill endyte.

2

My crewell fait, subjectit to penance,
predestinat sa void of all plesance,
has every greif amid myn hart ingrave.
The slyd inconstant destany or chance
unequaly doith hyng in thair ballance
my demeritis and gret dolour I have.

---

groundit, based, set. *frele*, frail. *regrait*, sorrow.
involupit, enveloped. *syte*, sorrow. *diffound*, pour out.
tyte, quickly, swiftly. *slyd*, slippery, *hyng*, hang.

40

This purgatory redowblys all the lave.
Ilk wycht has sum weilfare at obeysance
save me, bysnyng, that may na grace ressave.
Dede, thee addresse, and do me to my grave.

                    3

Wo worth sik strang mysforton anoyus,
quhilk has opprest my spretis maist joyus!
Wo worth this worldis freuch felicite!
Wo worth my fervent diseis dolorus!
Wo worth the wycht that is not pietuus,
quhare the trespassor penitent thay se!
Wo worth this dede that dayly dois me de!
Wo worth Cupid, and wo worth fals Venus!
Wo worth thaym bayth! Ay waryit mot thay be!
Wo worth thair court and cursyt destane!

---

bysnyng, monster. *thee addresse*, present yourself. *Wo worth*,
accursed be. *freuch*, frail, weak. *ay waryit mot thay be*, may
they be eternally cursed.

Palice of Honour, 607–36. The text is based on the
London edition, printed by William Copland *c.*1553,
as edited by Mrs Priscilla J. Bawcutt *The Shorter Poems
of Gavin Douglas* (*STS*, Edinburgh and London 1967),
pp. 44–6. One reading has been adopted from the
Edinburgh edition, printed by John Ross for Henry
Charteris in 1579. The poem was completed in 1501,
when Douglas was parson of Glenholm (Glenquhom)
in Peeblesshire. The title is taken from Copland's
marginal notes.

1.7. Charteris *involupit in syte*. Copland *involvit in
dispyte*.

XVIII

A ballat for Venus plesour

1

UNWEMMYT wit, deliverit of dangear,
maist happely preservit fra the snare,
releschit fre of service and bondage,
expell dolour, expell diseyses sare,
avoid displesour, womentyng and care,
ressave plesans and do thy sorowe swage,
behald thy glaid fresche lusty grene curage,
rejois amid thir lovers lait and air,
provide a place till plant thy tendir age,
quhair thou in joy and plesour may repair.

2

Quha is in welth, quha is weill fortunat,
quha is in peace, dissoverit from debbat,
quha levys in hop, quha levys in esperance,
quha standis in grace, quha standis in ferme estat,
quha is content, rejosyt air and lat,
or quha is he that Fortune doith avance,
bot thou that is replenyst with plesance?

---

unwemmyt, unharmed. *releschit*, released. *womentyng*, lamentatio
do thy sorowe swage, make your sorrow grow less violent.
dissoverit, separated. *ferme*, firm. *air and lat*, early and late.

42

Thou hes comfort, all weilfare dilligat,
thou hes gladnes, thou hes the happy chance,
thou hes thy will, now be not dissolat!

3

Incres in mirthfull consolatioun,
in joyus swete ymaginatioun.
Habond in luif of purifyit amouris.
With diligent trew deliberatioun
rendir lovyngis for thy salvatioun
till Venus, and ondir hir gard all houris.
Rest at all ease but sair or sytful schouris.
Abide in quiet maist constant weilfare.
Be glaid, and lycht now in thy lusty flouris,
unwemmyt wit, delyverit of dangare.

---

dilligat, delicate. *Habond in luif of purifyit amouris*, increase in
love of a purified, courtly kind. *lovyngis*, praises.
sytful, sorrowful. *lycht*, alight.

Palice of Honour, 1015–44. The text is again based on
Copland as edited by Mrs Bawcutt.

XIX

Tayis Bank

1

QUHEN Tayis bank wes blumyt brycht
with blosomes blyth and bred,
be that rever ran I doun rycht:
undir the rys I red.
The merle melit with all hir mycht
and mirth in mornyng maid.
Throw solace sound and semely sicht
alsuth a sang I said.

2

Undir that bank quhair blis had bene
I bownit me to abide.
Ane holene, hevinly hewit grene,
rycht heyndly did me hyd.
The sone schyne our the schawis schene
full semely me besyd.

---

bred, broad, wide. *rys*, bough. *red*, rode. *merle*, blackbird.
melit, mingled, joined (notes). *alsuth*, at once, immediately.
bownit me, prepared myself. *holene*, holly tree.
heyndly, courteously, graciously, pleasantly. *schyne*, shone.
schawis, groves. *schene*, beautiful.

ANONYMOUS

In bed of blumes bricht besene
a sleip couth me ourslyd.

3

About all blomet wes my bour
with blosummes broun and blew,
ourfret with mony fair fresch flour
helsum of hevinly hew
with schakeris of the schene dew schour
schynnyng my courtenis schew,
arrayit with a rich vardour
of Natouris werkis new.

4

Rasing the birdis fra thair rest,
the reid sone rais with rawis:
the lark sang loud quhill lycht mycht lest
a lay of luvis lawis:
the nythingall woik of hir nest
singing 'The day updawis';
the mirthfull maveis merriest
schill schowttit throw the schawis.

5

All flouris grew that firth within
that man couth haif in mind,
and in that flud all fische with fin
that creat wer be Kind.

---

besene, arrayed. *couth*, did. *ourslyd*, slide over. *ourfret*, adorned.
helsum, wholesome. *schakeris*, quivering. *courtenis*, curtains.
vardour, verdure. *rawis*, beams. *updawis*, dawns. *maveis*, thrush.
schill, shrill, *firth*, wood, grove. *couth*, could.

ANONYMOUS

Undir the rise the ra did ryn
our ron, our rute, our rind.
The dun deir dansit with a din,
and herdis of hairt and hind.

6

Wod Winter with his wallowand wind
but weir away wes went.
Brasit about with wild wodbynd
wer bewis on the bent.
Allone under the lusty lind
I saw ane lusum lent
that fairly war so fare to find
undir the firmament.

7

Scho wes the lustiest on live
allone lent on a land,
and farest figour be sic syve
that evir in firth I fand
hir cumly cullour to discryve
I dar nocht tak on hand.
Moir womanly borne of a wife
wes never, I dar warrand.

---

ra, roe. *ron*, small stream. *rind*, bark. *wod*, mad, angry.
wallowand, wallowing, gusty. *weir*, doubt.
brasit, embraced. *bent*, open ground, field. *lusum*, lovesome.
lent, lingering, tarrying. (I saw a lovesome one lingering).
fairly, wonder (as whom it would be a wonder to find so fair
a one under the firmament). *on a land*, on land.
be sic syve, by far (lit. by seven such). *discryve*, describe.
tak on hand, undertake.

46

8

To creatur that wes in cair,
or cauld of crewelty,
a blicht blenk of hir vesage bair
of baill his bute mycht be.
Hir hyd, hir hew, hir hevinly hair
mycht havy hairtis uphie.
So angelik under the air
never wicht I saw with e.

9

The blosummes that wer blyth and bricht
by hir wer blacht and blew.
Scho gladit all the foull of flicht
that in the forrest flew.
Scho mycht haif comfort king or knycht
that ever in cuntre I knew,
as waill and well of warldly wicht
in womanly vertew.

10

Hir cullour cleir, hir countinance,
hir cumly cristall ene,
hir portratour of most plesance,
all pictour did prevene.
Off every vertew to avance
quhen ladeis prasit bene,
rychttest in my remmembrance
that rose is rutit grene.

---

blicht, blythe. *blenk*, glance. *bute*, help, remedy. *uphie*, uplift.
blacht, bleached, pale. *waill*, choice, pick. *portratour*, figure.
prevene, surpass, *avance*, commend, praise.

11

This mild meik mansuet Margrite,
this perle polist most quhyt,
Dame Natouris deir dochter discreit,
the dyamant of delyt,
never formit wes to found on feit
ane figour moir perfyte,
nor non on mold that did hir meit
mycht mend hir wirth a mite.

12

This mirthfull maid to meit I ment
and merkit furth on mold,
but sone within a wane scho went,
most hevinly to behold.
The bricht sone with his bemys blent
upoun the bertis bold,
farest under the firmament
that formit wes on fold.

13

As parradice that place but peir
wes plesand to my sicht,
of forrest and of fresch reveir,
of firth and fowll of flicht,

---

mansuet, gentle. *Margrite*, both 'Margaret' and 'pearl'.
found, go, travel (found on feit, an alliterative tag).
on mold, on earth. *mend*, improve. *wirth a mite*, in any way
(lit. worth a mite). *ment*, attempted. *merkit furth*, moved
forward. *wane*, dwelling, palace. *blent*, glanced.
bertis, breast works, parapets. *on fold*, on earth.
reveir, river bank.

of birdis bay on bonk and breir
with blumes brekand bricht,
as hevin in to this erd doun heir,
hertis to hald on hicht.

14

So went this womanly away
amang thir woddis wyd,
and I to heir thir birdis gay
did in a bonk abyd,
quhair ron and rys rais in aray
endlang the rever syd.
This hapnit me in a time in May,
in till a morning tyd.

15

The rever throw the rise couth rowt,
and roseris rais on raw.
The schene birdis full schill couth schowt
into that semly schaw.
Joy wes within and joy without
under that wlonkest waw,
quhair Tay ran doun with stremis stout
full strecht under Stobschaw.

---

bay, song. *bonk*, bank. *breir*, briar-bush. *on hicht*, aloft. *rowt*, roar.
roseris, rose-bushes (and rose bushes rose in a row).
wlonkest, fairest. *waw*, wall. *strecht*, straight.

Bannatyne CCLXXVIII, f.229 a–b. The reference in
the poem is almost certainly to Lady Margaret Drummond, the eldest daughter of John Drummond, Lord
of that ilk and of Stobhall in Perthshire. In 1496 she

became mistress of James IV. She, together with her two sisters, was poisoned in 1502, some nine months before James's marriage to the English princess Margaret. 'All three were buried in the choir of Dunblane Cathedral, beneath three great blue stones, which may be seen to this day. Though there is probably no truth in the legend that James had set his heart on marrying her, but had been forced to yield to the opposition of the nobles, who wished him to marry an English princess, and of the clergy, who declared that the lovers stood within the forbidden degrees of kinship, it is certain that he did not regard her as a mere light of love. He ordered dirges to be sung for her in Edinburgh, and year after year he feed two priests to say masses in Dunblane Cathedral for the repose of her soul' (R.L. Mackie *King James IV of Scotland* (Edinburgh and London 1958) pp. 100–1.

ANONYMOUS

XX

1

QUHEN FLORA had ourfret the firth
in May, of every moneth quene;
quhen merle and mavis singis with mirth,
sweit melling in the schawis schene;
quhen all luvaris rejosit bene
and most desyrus of thair pray,
I hard a lusty luvar mene,
'I luve bot I dar nocht assay.

2

Strang ar the panis I daylie prufe,
bot yit with pacience I sustene,
I am so fetterit with the lufe
onlie of my lady schene,
quhilk for hir bewty mycht be quene,
natour sa craftely alwey
hes done depaint that sweit serene.
Quhome I luf, I dar nocht assay.

---

ourfret, adorned, decorated. *firth,* wood, *merle,* blackbird.
mavis, thrush. *melling,* joining. *schawis,* groves. *schene,* beautiful.
mene, complain.

ANONYMOUS

3

Scho is so brycht of hyd and hew,
I lufe bot hir allone, I wene.
Is non hir luf that may eschew,
that blenkis of that dulce amene,
so cumly cleir at hir twa ene
that scho ma luvaris dois effrey
than evir of Grice did fair Helene.
Quhom I luve, I dar nocht assay.'

---

blenkis of, glances at. *dulce*, sweet, pleasant to the sight.
amene, agreeable, pleasing one. *effrey*, terrify. *Grice*, Greece.

Bannatyne CCLI, f.218a.

ANONYMOUS

XXI

1

O LUSTY May with Flora quene!
The balmy dropis frome Phebus schene
preluciand bemes befoir the day.
Be that Diana growis grene
throwch glaidnes of this lusty May.

2

Than Esperus that is so bricht
till wofull hairtis castis his lycht
with bankis that blumes on every bray,
and schuris ar sched furth of thair sicht
thruch glaidnes of this lusty May.

3

Birdis on bewis of every birth
rejosing nottis makand thair mirth
rycht plesandly upoun the spray

---

preluciand, both 'shining brightly' and 'shining before'.
Diana, the wood, the forest (Diana was a wood-goddess.
See *The Oxford Classical Dictionary*). *Esperus*, here, the Morning
Star. *bray*, the face of a hill. *schuris ar sched furth of thair sicht*,
they cease to weep. *bewis*, boughs. *of every birth*, of every rank,
kind. *nottis*, notes, song.

with flurissingis our feild and firth
thruch glaidnes of this lusty May.

4

All luvaris that ar in cair
to thair ladeis thay do repair
in fresch mornyngis befoir the day,
and ar in mirth ay mair and mair
thruch glaidnes of this lusty May.

---

flurissingis, flourishes, decorative additions
introduced by player or singer.

Bannatyne CCLXXIX, f.229b. One should not miss the
generally learned and humanistic tone of the poem as a
whole. It is mentioned in *The Complaynt of Scotlande*
(1549). See footnote 9, p. lxx.

ANONYMOUS

XXII

1

ALLACE depairting, grund of wo
thou art, of everilk joy ane end!
How suld I perte my lady fro?
How suld I tak my leif to wend?
Sen fals Fortoun is nocht my frend,
bot evir castis me to keill,
now, sen I most no langir lend,
I tak my leif aganis my will.

2

Fairweill, fairweill, my weilfair may,
fairweill, fegour most fresche of hew,
fairweill, the saiffar of assay,
fairweill, the hart of quhyt and blew,
fairweill, baith kynd, curtas and trew,
fairweill, woman withowttin ill,
fairweill, the cumlest that evir I knew.
I tak my leif aganis my will.

3

Fairweill, my rycht fair lady deir,
fairweill, most wys and womanlie,
fairweill, my lufe fro yeir to yeir,

---

grund, cause. *castis*, plans. *keill*, kill. *lend*, stay. *may*, maiden.
saiffar, sapphire. *assay*, proved or tried value.
quhyt and blew, i. e. faith and steadfastness.

ANONYMOUS

fairweill, thou beriall blycht of blie,
fairweill, leill lady liberall and fre,
fairweill, that may me saif and spill.
Fowevir I fair, go fair weill ye.
I tak my leif aganis my will.

4

Fairweill fra me, my gudly grace,
fairweill, the well of wirdines,
fairweill, my confort in everilk place,
fairweill, the hoip of steidfastnes,
fairweill, the rute of my distres,
fairweill, the luffar trew and still,
fairweill, the nureis of gentilnes.
I tak my leif aganis my will.

---

blycht, happy, glad. *blie*, colour, complexion. *leill*, faithful.
spill, put to death. *fowevir*, N.E. dialect form of 'howevir'.
wirdines, worthiness. *nureis*, nurse, 'nourice'.

Bannatyne CCLXVIII, f.225a–b. See Introduction,
pp. xxviii–xxx.

XXIII

1

MY TREWTH is plicht unto my lufe benyng
that meit and sleip is quyt bereft me fro.
With luvaris mo of murnyng I may sing
without glaidnes, quhair evir I ryd or go.
And I hir freind, quhy suld scho be my fo?
Do as scho list, I do me in hir cure
on to the deid to be hir serviture.

2

And thocht I dar nocht daly do present
hir for to serf for hurting of hir name,
I dreid the serpent sklander do hir schent.
Bot nevirtheles hir honour and hir fame
I sall keip in armis and in game
unto the time that Atropus the threid
sall cute of life bayth in word and deid.

3

O Cupeid king, thyn eiris now incline,
and pers my lady inwart to the hairt

---

and thocht . . . hir name, and though I dare not be present
each day to serve her for (fear of) hurting her name.
do hir schent, ruin her. *Atropus*, the third fury.

with that ilk dart that thou hes persit mine,
and caus hir so that scho to me revarte
for to haif mercy unto my pane and smarte,
or feill the pine that faithfull luvaris haif,
for, but hir lufe, I graith me to my graif.

---

revarte, turn back. *graith me to*, prepare myself for.

Bannatyne CCLXXXVIII, ff.234b–235a. For this and
the following poem, see Introduction pp. xxx–xxxiii.

XXIV

1

PANSING in hairt with spreit opprest this
    hindirnycht bygon,
my corps for walking wes molest for lufe only
    of on.
Allace, quhome to suld I mak mon, sen this
    come too lait?
Cauld, cauld culis the lufe that kendillis our het.

2

Hir bewty and hir maikles maik dois reif my
    spreit me fro,
and causis me no rest to tak bot tumlyng to
    and fro.
My curage than is hence ago, sen I may nocht
    hir gett.
Cauld, cauld culis the lufe that kendillis our het.

---

pansing, musing. *this hindirnycht bygon*, the other night.
corps, body. *walking*, waking. *culis*, cools. *kendillis*, kindles.
our, over, too. *het*, hot. *maikles*, matchless. *maik*, shape, form.
reif, take by violence (from).

3

Hir first to luf quhen I began, I trowd scho
    luvit me,
bot I, allace, wes nocht the man that best
    pleisit hir e.
Thairfoir will I lat dolour be and gang
    ane uther gett.
Cauld, cauld culis the lufe that kendillis our het.

4

First quhen I kest my fantesy, thair fermly
    did I stand,
and howpit weill that scho suld be all haill
    at my command.
Bot suddanly scho did ganestand and contrair
    maid debait.
Cauld, cauld culis the lufe that kendillis our het.

5

Hir proper makdome so perfyt, hir visage
    cleir of hew,
scho raissis on me sic appetite and causis
    me hir persew.
Allace, scho will nocht on me rew, nor gre
    with mine estait.
Cauld, cauld culis the lufe that kendillis our het.

---

gang ane uther gett, go another way. *kest*, cast, directed.
howpit, hoped. *ganestand*, oppose. *makdome*, comeliness, beaut
gre, agree.

6

Sen scho hes left me in distres, in dolour
   and in cair,
without I get sum uther grace, my life will
   lest no mair.
Scho is our proper trim and fair ane trew hairt
   to oursett.
Cauld, cauld culis the lufe that kendillis our het.

7

Suld I ly doun in havines, I think it is bot vane.
I will get up with merrines and cheis als
   gud agane,
foir I will maik to you plane, my hairt
   it is oursett.
Cauld, cauld culis the lufe that kendillis our het.

8

No, no, I will nocht trow as yit that scho
   will leif me so,
nor yit that scho will chenge or flit, as thocht
   scho be my fo.
Thairfoir will I lat dolour go and gang
   ane uthir gait.
Cauld, cauld culis the lufe that kendlis our het.

---

lest, last. *oursett*, overthrow. *cheis*, choose.

Bannatyne CCCIX, f.245a–b.

XXV

1

THIR lenterne dayis ar luvely lang,
and I will murne ne mair,
nor for no mirthles may me mang
that will not for me cair.
I wilbe glaid and latt hir gang
with falsat in hir fair.
I find ane freschar feir to fang
baith of hyd, hew and hair.

2

The wintter nycht is lang but weir.
I may murne gif I will.
Scho will not murne for me, that cleir,
thairfoir I wilbe still.
O King of Luve that is so cleir,
I me acquit you till.
Sa scho fra me and I fra hir,
and not bot it be skill.

---

lenterne dayis, days of Lent, spring. *me mang,* vex myself.
falsat, falsehood. *fair,* bearing, demeanour, conduct.
feir, mate, spouse. *fang,* embrace. *weir,* doubt. *skill,* that which
is reasonable (so may she go from me and I from her, and only
because it is reasonable).

3

O Lord of Luve, how lykis thee
my lemmens laitis unleill?
Scho luvis ane uthir bettir than me.
I haif caus to appeill.
I pray to him that deit on tre,
that for us all thold baill,
mot send my lemmane twa or thre,
sen scho can not be leill.

4

Uthir hes hir hairt. Sowld scho haif mine,
trewly that war grit wrang.
Quhen thay haif play, gif I haif pine,
on gallowis mot I hang:
or for hir luve gif I decline,
thocht scho evill nevir so lang,—
quhen I think on hir foirheid fine,
than mon I sing ane sang.

5

Off all the houris of the nycht
I can not tell you ane,
so murne I for my lady bricht
fro sleip haif me ourtane.

---

lemmens, lovers. *laitis*, ways, conduct. *unleill*, unfaithful.
appeill, make a legal appeal (at the court of the God of Love).
thold, suffered. *baill*, suffering, sorrow. *twa or thre*, (i.e. *baillis*,
sorrows). *thocht scho evill nevir so lang*, however long she has
thought ill (of me).

Fro scho be past out of my sicht
the casting of ane stane,
I haif no langour, be this licht
I love God of his lane.

6

Allace that evir fader me gat,
or moder me wend in clais,
gif I sowld for ane womans saik
my life thus leid in lais
for ye saw nevir so fair a caik
of meill that millar mais,
bot yit ane man wald get the maik.
As gud luve cumis as gais.

---

love, praise. *of his lane*, for his gift, loan (*I love God of his lane*,
Thank God for it!). *clais*, clothes. *in lais*, in captivity, bonda;
maik, equal.

Bannatyne CCCXXV, f.252a–b. For Stewart's career, see
D. Hamer *The Works of Sir David Lindsay* III (*STS*,
Edinburgh and London 1934), pp. 76–7.

XXVI

1

I AM AS I am and so will I be,
bot how that I am, nane knawis trewlie.
Be it ill, be it weill, be I bund, be I fre,
I am as I am and so will I be.

2

I leid my life indifferently.
I mene na thing bot honesty,
and thocht men juge dyversly,
I am as I am and so will I be.

3

I do nocht rew nor yit complane.
Baith mirth and sadnes I do refrane,
and use the folkis that can nocht fane.
I am as I am, be it plesour or pane.

4

Divers do juge as thay trow,
sum of plesour and sum of wo,
yit for all that no thing thay knaw.
I am as I am, quhair evir I go.

5

Bot sen that jugeris do tak that wey,
lat every man his judgment say.
I will it tak in sport and pley,
for I am as I am, quhaevir sa nay.

6

Quha jugeis weill, weill God him send.
Quha jugeis ill, God thame amend.
To juge the best thairfoir intend.
I am as I am and so will I end.

7

Yit sum thair be that takis delyt
to juge folkis thocht for invy and spyt.
Bot quhidder thay juge me wrang or ryt,
I am as I am and so will I wryt.

8

Praying you all that this dois reid
to trest it as ye do your creid,
and nocht to think that I chenge my weid.
I am as I am how evir I speid.

9

But how that is, I leif to you.
Juge as ye list, owdir fals or trew.
Ye knaw no moir than afoir ye knew.
I am as I am, quhat evir enschew.

10

And frome this mind I will nocht fle,
bot to you all that misjugeis me
I do protest, as ye may se,
that I am as I am and so will I be.

Bannatyne CCCXXII, f.250a–b. Compare Wyatt
Collected Poems, ed. Kenneth Muir (London 1949), pp.
154–5. Muir does not note the existence of a text in
Bannatyne.

SIR GEORGE CLAPPERTON *c.*1505–157

XXVII

1

IN BOWDOUN on Blak Monunday,
quhen all was gadderit to the play,
bayth men and women semblit thair,
I hard ane sweit ane sicht and say,
'Way worth maryage for evermair!

2

Madinis, ye may have grit plesance
for to do Venus observance,
thocht I inclusit be with cair
that I dar nother sing nor dance.
Wa worth maryage for evirmair!

Bowdoun, Bowden in Roxburghshire near St Boswells and
Dryburgh. Until the Reformation the church belonged to th
monks of Kelso Abbey. Pasche plays (Easter plays) were stil
being performed at Linton in the presbytery of Kelso in 161
See Anna J. Mill *Medieval Plays in Scotland* (Edinburgh and
London 1927) pp 257–60. *Blak Monunday*, Easter Monday.
gadderit, gathered. *play*, an Easter Monday performance of a
more or less dramatic kind. *semblit*, assembled. *hard*, heard.
wa worth, accursed be! *inclusit*, imprisoned.

68

3

Quhen that I was ane madein ying,
lichtlie wald I dance and sing
and sport and play bayth lait and air.
Now dar I nocht luik to sic thing.
Way wourth maryage for evirmair!

4

Thus am I bundin out of blis
on to ane churle sayis I am his,
that I dar nocht luik our the stair
Scantlie to gif sir Johne ane kis.
Wa worth maryage for evirmair!

5

Now war I ane madin as I wes,
to mak me lady of the Bas,
and thocht that I wer never so fair,
to weddin suld I never pas.
Way worth maryage for evirmair!

6

Thus am I thirlit on to ane schrew
quhilk dow nothing of chalmer glew,
off bowre bourding bayth bask and bair.
God wayt gif I have caus to rew!
Way wourth maryage for evirmair!

---

bundin, secured by bonds. *our*, over. *the stair*, the forestair
characteristic of Scottish domestic architecture. *scantlie*, merely.
sir Johne, a priest. *Bas*, the Bass Rock. *thirlit*, subjected to.
dow, is worth. *chalmer glew*, chamber sport, lovemaking.
bowre bourding, sport in a lady's private apartment.
bask, unpleasant.

7

All nicht I clatter upoin my creid,
prayand to God gif I wer deid,
or ellis out of this warld I wair.
Than suld I se for sum remeid.
Way wourth maryage for evirmair!

8

Ye suld heir tell, and he wer gane,
that I suld be ane wantoun ane
to leir the law of luiffis layr.
In our toun lyk me suld be nane.
Way worth maryage for evirmair!

9

I suld put on my russet gowne,
my reid kirtill, my hois of broun,
and lat thame se my yallow hair
undir my curche hingand doun.
Way wourth maryage for evirmair!

10

Luffairis bayth suld heir and se
I suld luif thame that wald luif me.
Thair hartis for me suld never be sair.
Bot ay unweddit suld I be.
Way wourth maryage for evirmair!'

---

clatter upoin my creid, repeat the Creed continually (tell my beads
curche, kerchief. *hingand,* hanging.

Maitland Folio LXXIX. See Introduction, pp. xxxiii–xxxiv. A
good example of the *chanson à mal mariée.*

XXVIII

1

LANTERNE of lufe and lady fair of hew,
O perle of price, most precius and preclair,
O dasy duls, gayest that evir grew,
off every wicht most sweit and singulare,
O flour delyce most flurisand and fair,
unto this taill, sweit turtor, thou attend:
my thirlit hairt so law in to dispair
unto thy mercy I meikly me commend.

2

O jem of joy injonit in my hairt,
O plant of prys most plesand and perfyte,
the rycht remeid of all my panis smarte,
my spreit is reft to se thy cullour quhyte
devoid of wo, of sorrow and of syte
quhois bewteis all no hairt may comprehend:
my visage wan, O lady of delyte,
unto thy mercy I meikly me commend.

3

Sen thou art scho that hes my hairt in cure,
my howp, my heill, my weill and eik my wo,

---

preclair, very beautiful, *duls*, sweet. *singulare*, unique, eminent.
turtor, turtle-dove. *thirlit*, pierced. *injonit in*, united to.
plant of prys, i.e., rare medicinal herb. *syte*, sorrow.

lat me nocht swerf, your hummill serviture,
for but remeid my hairt will brist in two.
Now lady fair, my freind and eik my fo,
quhom on but dowt all vertew dois depend,
my hairt and mind, quhair evir I ryd or go,
unto thy mercy meikly I me commend.

---

swerf, swoon, faint.

Bannatyne CCLXXXIX, f.235a. See Introduction,
pp. xxxiv–xxxv. The poem is clearly addressed to
someone called Margaret.

XXIX

1

HAIF hairt in hairt, ye hairt of hairtis haill.
Trewly, sweit hairt, your hairt my hairt sal haif.
Expell, deir hairt, my havy hairtis baill,
praying you, hairt quhilk hes my hairt in graif,
sen ye, sweit hairt, my hairt may sla and saif,
lat nocht, deir hairt, my leill hairt be forloir,
excelland hairt of every hairtis gloir.

2

Glad is my hairt with you, sweit hairt, to rest
and serve you, hairt, with hairtis observance.
Sen ye ar, hairt, with bayth our hairtis possest,
my hairt is in your hairtis governance.
Do with my hairt your hairtis sweit plesance,
for is my hairt thrall your hairt untill.
I haif no hairt contrair your hairtis will.

3

Sen ye haif, hairt, my faithfull hairt in cure,
uphald the hairt quhilk is your hairtis awin.
Gif my hairt be your hairtis serviture,
how may ye thoill your trew hairt be
    ourthrawin?

---

hairt of hairtis haill, heart of all hearts.
baill, suffering, sorrow. *graif*, grave, tomb. *forloir*, lost.
awin, own. *thoill*, endure, bear.

Quhairfoir, sweit hairt, nocht suffer so be
    knawin,
bot ye be, hairt, my hairtis rejosing,
as ye ar hairt of hairtis conforting.

Bannatyne CCLXXV, f.228a. Bannatyne has a marginal
note, which is repeated in the colophon, 'The answeir
heirof in the 235 leif', a reference to Alexander Scott's
poem, 'Considdir, hairt, my trew intent' (no. XXXVII
of the present collection.) See Introduction, p. lii.

ALEXANDER SCOTT *c*.1515–*c*.1583

XXX

1

IT CUMIS you luvaris to be laill,
off body, hairt and mind alhaill,
and thocht ye with your ladyis daill,
      ressoun,
bot and your faith and lawty faill,
      tressoun.

2

Ye may with honesty persew,
gif ye be constant, trest and trew.
Thocht than unrycht thay on you rew,
      ressoun,
bot be ye fund dowbill—adew!
      Tressoun.

3

Your hummill service first resing thame,
for that to your intent sall bring thame.
With leif of ladeis thocht ye thing thame,
      ressoun,
bot eftirwart and ye maling thame,
      tressoun.

---

cumis, becomes, behoves. *laill*, loyal, faithful. *daill*, meddle.
lawty, loyalty. *trest*, trusty. *unrycht*, wrongly, foolishly.
resing, resign, hand over. *thing*, have intercourse with.

4

Do nevir the deid that ma diseis thame,
bot wirk with all your mind to meis thame.
To tak your plesour quhen it pleis thame,
  ressoun,
bot with untrewth and ye betrais thame,
  tressoun.

5

Defend thair fame, quha evir fyle thame,
and ay with honest havingis style thame,
to Venus als suppois ye wile thame,
  ressoun,
bot be ye fraudfull and begyle thame,
  tressoun.

6

Ye suld considdir or ye taik thame,
that littill service will nocht staik thame.
Get ye ane goldin hour to glak thame,
  ressoun,
bot be ye fraudfull and forsaik thame,
  tressoun.

---

diseis, vex (but also 'disease'?). *meis*, soothe. *betrais*, betray.
fyle, stain, slander. *havingis*, behaviour.
staik, suit. *glak*, toy with.

7

Be secreit, trew and plane allwey.
Defend thair fame baith nycht and day,
in prevy place suppois ye play—
      ressoun,
bot be ye ane clattrer, harmisay!
      Tressoun.

8

Be courtas in thair cumpany,
for that sall caus thame to apply,
thocht that thay lat you with thame ly—
      ressoun,
bot be ye fund unfaithfull, fy!
      Tressoun.

9

Wey weill thir versis that I wryt you.
Do your devoir quhen that thay lat you.
To lufe your ladeis, quho can wyt you?
      Ressoun.
Do ye the contrair, heir I quyt you.
      Tressoun.

---

harmisay, alas! *apply*, hear, listen. *devoir*, duty. *wyt*, blame.
quyt, disown, renounce.

Bannatyne CCXCIII, ff.236b–237a. For this and the
following poems by Scott, see Introduction, pp. xlvi–lxiii.

XXXI

1

LUVE preysis but comparesone
both gentill, sempill, generall,
and of fre will gevis waresone,
as Fortoun chansis to befall,
for luve makis nobill ladeis thrall
to bassir men of birth and blud:
so luve garris sobir wemen small
get maistrice our grit men of gud.

2

Ferme luve for favour, feir or feid,
of riche nor pur to speik suld spair,
for luve to hienes hes no heid,
nor lychtleis lawlines ane air,
but puttis all personis in compair,
this proverb planely for till preve,
that men and wemen, les and mair,
ar cumd of Adame and of Eve.

---

preysis, subdues. *but comparesone*, incomparably (?without
distinction). *generall*, i.e. 'everyone'. *waresone*, award, reward.
maistrice, mastery. *feid*, enmity. *hes no heid*, has no heed.
lychtleis, despises. *air*, jot, particle (?hair). *in compair*, on a level.

3

So, thocht my liking wer a leddy,
and I no lord, yit nocht the les
scho suld my service find als reddy
as duke to duches docht him dres.
For as proud princely luve expres
is to haif soverenitie,
so service cumis of sympilnes,
and leilest lufe of law degre.

4

So luvaris lair no leid suld lak,
a lord to lufe a silly las,
a leddy als for luf to tak
ane proper page, hir time to pas,
for quhy as bricht bene birneist bras
as silver wrocht at all devys,
and als gud drinking out of glas
as gold, thocht gold gif grittar prys.

5

Suld I presome this sedull schaw,
or lat me langouris be lamentit?
Na—I effrey for feir and aw
hir comlie heid be miscontenttit.

---

liking, love. *docht*, could. *him dress*, address himself, offer himself.
leilest, most faithful. *lair*, lore. *leid*, person (*no leid*, no one).
for quhy, because. *bene*, is. *birneist*, burnished.
at all devys, elaborately. *sedull*, letter, poem.
I effrey, I'm afraid.

I dar nocht preis hir to present it,
for, be scho wreth, I will nocht vow it,
bot pleiss hir prowdens to imprent it,
scho may persave sum Inglis throw it.

———————————————————————

preis, draw near. *vow*, avow. *imprent*, fix firmly in the mind.

XXXII

1

Up, helsum hairt, thy rutis rais and lowp,
exalt and clym within my breist in staige.
Art thou nocht wantoun, haill and in gud howp,
fermit in grace and free of all thirlaige,
bathing in blis and sett in hie curaige,
braisit in joy? No falt may thee affray,
having thy ladeis hart as heretaige
in blenche ferme for ane sallat every May.
So neidis thou nocht now sussy, sytt nor sorrow,
sen thou art sure of sollace evin and morrow.

2

Thou, Cupeid king, rewardit me with this.
I am thy awin trew liege without tressone.
Thair levis no man in moir eis, welth and blis.
I knaw no siching, sadnes nor yit soun,
walking, thocht, langour, lamentatioun,
dolor, dispair, weiping nor jelosye.
My breist is void and purgit of pussoun.
I feill no pane. I haif no purgatorye,
bot peirles, perfytt, paradisall plesour,
with mirry hairt and mirthfulnes but mesoure.

---

helsum, vigorous, joyful. *lowp*, leap. *clym . . . in staige*, mount
aloft. *howp*, hope. *fermit*, established. *thirlaige*, vassalage.
braisit, firmly secured. *blenche ferme*, nominal rent.
sallat, salad. *sussy*, care. *sytt*, grieve.
soun, faintness. *pussoun*, poison.

3

My lady, lord, thou gaif me for to hird,
Within mine armes I nureis on the nycht.
Kissing, I say 'My bab, my tendir bird,
sweit maistres, lady luffe and lusty wicht,
steir, rewll and gyder of my sensis richt.'
My voice surmontis the sapheir cludis hie,
thanking grit God of that tressour and micht.
I coft hir deir, bot scho fer derrer me,
quhilk hasard honor, fame in aventeur,
committing clene hir corse to me in cure.

4

In oxteris clois we kis and cossis hairtis,
brynt in desire of amouris play and sport,
meittand oure lustis. Spreitles we twa depertis.
Prolong with lasir, lord, I thee exhort,
sic time that we may boith tak our confort,
first for to sleip, syne walk without espyis.
I blame the cok. I plene the nicht is schort.
Away I went. My wache the cuschett cryis,
wissing all luvaris leill to haif sic chance
that thay may haif us in remembrance.

---

hird, tend, watch over. *steir*, pilot. *coft*, bought. *oxteris*, arms.
cossis, exchange. *brynt*, burnt. *espyis*, spys. *plene*, complain.
went, wend, go. *cuschett*, cushat, ring dove.

Bannatyne CCCIII, ff.242b–243a.

2.1. Cupeid king, MS *Cupeid*.

XXXIII

1

Rycht as the glas bene thirlit thrucht with bemis
of Phebus fair prefulgent visage bricht,
or hornit Dyane with hir paly glemis
persis the cluddis sabill in the nicht,
and as the kocatrice keilis with hir sicht,
rycht so the bewty of my lady stoundis
outthrowcht my breist, unto my hairt
    redoundis.

2

Behaild how far cristall or diamant,
jassink, jasp, ruby, jem or criselleit,
carbunkile, emmerauld, perle or athamant,
turcas, topas, marbill or margareit
exceidis the barrat stonis in the streit;
in lyk wayis dois hir bewty undegraid
transcend all uthiris, wife, wedow or maid.

---

thirlit, pierced, penetrated. *keilis*, kills.
stoundis, thrills, shoots. *jassink*, jacinth.
athamant, adamant, diamond. *margareit*, pearl.
barrat, common, ordinary. *undegraid*, matchless, peerless.

3

Espy richt so how far the rosy gowlis
pasis the wallowit weidis in the vaill,
or sound of lark aboif the revenous fowlis,
and somersday the nichtis hiemaill,
or as ane galay gayest undir saill
bene plesandar nor taikles boitis small,
so is my lady lustiest of all.

---

gowlis, marigolds. *wallowit*, withered, faded.
revenous, ravenous (*revenous fowlis*, birds of prey).
hiemaill, winter. *taikles*, tackleless, without sailing gear.

Bannatyne CCCI, f.239b.

84

XXXIV

1

QUHA is perfyte to put in wryt
the inwart murnyng and mischance,
or to indite the grit delyte
of lustie lufis observance,
bot he that may certane patiently suffir pane
to win his soverane in recompance?

2

Albeid I knaw of luvis law
the plesour and the panis smart,
yit I stand aw for to furthschaw
the quiet secreitis of my harte,
for it may Fortoun raith to do hir body skaith
quhilk wait that of thame baith I am expert.

3

Scho wait my wo, that is ago;
scho wait my weilfair and remeid;
scho wait also I lufe no mo
bot hir, the well of womanheid;
scho wait withouttin faill I am hir luvar laill:
scho hes my hairt alhaill till I be deid.

---

raith, anger. *skaith*, harm. *baith*, i.e.. 'the plesour and the
panis smart'.

4

That bird of blis in bewty is
in erd the only *A per se*
quhais mouth to kis is worth, I wis,
the warld full of gold to me.
Is nocht in erd I cure bot pleis my lady pure,
syne be hir serviture unto I de.

5

Scho hes my lufe. At hir behufe
my hairt is subject, bound and thrall,
for scho dois moif my hairt aboif
to se hir proper persoun small.
Sen scho is wrocht at will, that natur may fulfill,
glaidly I gif hir till body and all.

6

Thair is nocht wie can estimie
my sorrow and my sichingis sair,
for so am I done fathfullie
in favouris with my lady fair,
that baith our hairtis ar ane, luknyt in
    luvis chene,
and everilk greif is gane for evir mair.

---

wie, man, person. *luknyt*, locked up.

Bannatyne CCXCII, f.236a–b.

6.3. so am I, MS *I/am so*, where the oblique indicates
that *I* is the rhyming syllable.

XXXV

1

Lo, quhat it is to lufe!
Lerne, ye that list to prufe,
be me, I say, that no ways may
the grund of greif remufe,
bot still decay both nycht and day.
Lo, quhat it is to lufe!

2

Lufe is ane fervent fire
kendillit without desire,
schort plesour, lang displesour.
Repentence is the hire,
ane pure tressour without mesour.
Lufe is ane fervent fire.

3

To lufe and to be wyis,
to rege with gud advyis,
now thus, now than, so gois the game:
incertane is the dyis.
Thair is no man, I say, that can
both lufe and to be wyis.

---

kendillit, kindled. *without desire*, unsolicited, unsought.
hire, wage, reward. *pure*, poor.

SCOTT

4

Fle alwayis frome the snair.
Lerne at me to be ware.
It is ane pane and dowbill trane
of endles wo and cair.
For to refrane that denger plane
fle alwayis frome the snair.

---

refrane, escape, avoid.

Bannatyne CCCLXXV, f.286a–b.

88

XXXVI

The lament of the Maister of Erskine

I

DEPERTE, deperte, deperte—allace, I most
    deperte
frome hir that hes my hart with hart full soir,
aganis my will in deid, and can find no remeid.
I wait the panis of deid can do no moir.

2

Now most I go, allace, frome sicht of hir
    sweit face,
the grund of all my grace and soverane.
Quhat chans that may fall me, sall I nevir
    mirry be
unto the time I se my sweit agane.

3

I go and wait nocht quhair, I wandir heir
    and thair,
I weip and sichis rycht sair with panis smart.
Now most I pas away, away, in wildirnes and
    wilsum way.
Allace! this wofull day we suld depairte.

---

wilsum, dreary.

4

My spreit dois quaik for dreid, my thirlit
    hairt dois bleid,
my panis dois exceid—quhat suld I say,
I, wofull wycht allone, makand ane
    petous mone?
Allace! my hairt is gone for evir and ay.

5

Throw langour of my sweit, so thirlit is
    my spreit
my dayis ar most compleit throw hir absence.
Christ sen scho knew my smert ingravit in
    my hairt,
becaus I most deperte frome hir presens.

6

Adew! my awin sweit thing, my joy and
    comforting,
my mirth and sollesing of erdly gloir.
Fair weill, my lady bricht and my remem-
    brance rycht,
fair weill and haif gud nycht. I say no moir.

---

thirlit, pierced, penetrated. *langour of*, languor for. *most compleit*
ended. *sen*, grant.

Bannatyne CCCX, ff.245b–246a. The title is based on the
colophon, 'Quod Scott off the Maister of Erskyn'. See
Introduction, pp. xxxviii, and compare Knox's *History
of the Reformation* (ed. Croft Dickinson, I, 101): 'In that
same battle was slain the Master of Erskine, dearly
beloved of the Queen [Mary of Guise] for whom she
made great lamentation, and bore his death many days
in mind.' The Master was killed at Pinkie in 1547.

XXXVII

The answeir to the ballat of hairtis

1

CONSIDDIR, hairt, my trew intent,
suppois I am nocht eloquent
to wryt you anser responsive:
your scedull is so excellent
it pasis far my wittis five,

2

For quhy it is so full of hairtis
that mine within my bosum stairtis
quhen I behald it rycht till end,
and for ilk hairt ane hundreth dertis
outthrow my hairt to you I send.

3

This woundit hairt, sweit hairt, ressaif
quhilk is, deir hairt, abone the laif,
your faithfull hairt with trew intent;
ane trewar hairt may no man haif
nor yit ane hairt moir permanent.

4

Ane hairt it is without dissait.
It is the hairt to quhome ye wret
the misseif full of hairtis seir.
It is ane hairt bayth air and lait
that is your hairtis presoneir.

5

It is ane hairt full of distres,
ane cairfull hairt all comfortles,
ane penseve hairt in dule and dolour,
ane hairt of wo and havines,
ane mirthles hairt withouttin mesour.

6

It is ane hairt bayth firme and stabill,
ane hairt withouttin fenyeit fabill,
ane constant hairt, bayth trest and trew,
ane sure hairt set in to sabill,
ane wofull hairt bot gif ye rew.

7

It is ane hairt that your hairt servis,
ane hairt for lufe of your hairt stervis,
ane hairt that nevir you offendit,
ane hairt of youris, bayth vane and nervis,
ane hairt but solace bot gif ye send it.

---

wret, wrote. *seir*, many. *fenyeit*, feigned, false, hypocritical.
stervis, dies, perishes.

8

It is na gravit hairt in stone,
in silver, gold nor evir bone,
nor yit ane payntit symlitud,
bot this same verry hairt allone
within my breist of flesch and blude.

9

Thairfoir, sweit hairt, send me the hairt
that is in to your breist inwart,
and nocht thir writtin hairtis in vane,
bot your hairt to my hairt revert
and send me hairt for hairt agane.

---

gravit, graven, engraved (i.e. on an ornament).
evir bone, ivory. *revert*, turn, change.

Bannatyne CCXCI, ff.235b–236a. This poem was
written in answer to no. XXIX. The title is taken
from Bannatyne's marginal note.

5.5. withouttin, MS *without*. So in 6.2.

XXXVIII

1

OPPRESSIT hairt, indure in dolour and distres,
wappit without recure in wo remidiles.
Sen scho is merciles and causis all thy smert
quhilk suld thy dolour dres, indure,
    oppressit hairt.

2

Perfors tak paciens and dre thy destany.
To lufe but recompens is grit perplexitie.
Of thine adversitie wyt thy self and no mo,
for quhen that thou wes fre, thou wald nocht
    hald thee so.

3

Thou langit ay to prufe the strenth of luvis lair,
and quhatkin thing wes lufe quhilk now
    settis thee so sair.
Off all thy wo and cair it mendis thee nocht
    to mene—
howbeid thou suld forfair, thyself the
    caus hes bene.

---

wappit, wrapped. *dres*, redress. *lair*, instruction
quhatkin, what kind of. *mene*, complain.
forfair, perish.

4

Quhen thou wes weill at eis and subject to
    no wicht,
thou hir for lufe did cheis quhilk settis thy lufe
    at licht,
and thocht thou knew hir slicht, yit wald thou
    nocht refrane:
thairfoir it is bot rycht that thou indure the pane.

5

Bot yit my corps, allace, is wrangusly opprest
be thee into this cace and brocht to grit wanrest.
Quhy suld it so be drest be thee and daly pynd
quhilk still it ay detest, thy wantoun folich
    mind?

6

The blenkyne of ane e ay gart thee goif and
    glaik.
My body bad lat be and of thy siching slaik.
Thou wald nocht rest bot raik and lair thee
    in the mire.
Yit felyeit thou to faik that thou did maist
    desire.

---

slicht, fickle, worthless. *wanrest*, trouble. *drest*, treated.
blenkyne, wanton twinkle. *goif*, gaze, stare.
glaik, look foolishly. *raik*, roam, range.
lair, stick. *felyeit*, failed. *faik*, grasp.

7

Thocht thou do murn and weip with inwart
    spreit opprest,
quhen uthir men takis sleip, thou wantis the
    nychtis rest,
scho quhome thou luvis best, off thee takis
    littill thocht:
thy wo and grit wanrest and cair scho countis
    nocht.

8

Thairfoir go hens in haist my langour to lament:
do nocht my body waist quhilk nevir did
    consent,
and thocht thou wald repent that thou hir hes
    persewit,
yit man thou stand content and drink that
    thou hes brewit.

Bannatyne CCCXIII, ff.246b–247a. See Introduction,
pp. lii–liii.

4.3. nocht refrane, MS *refrane*. The emendation was
suggested in the Hunterian Club edition.

XXXIX

1

HENCE, hairt, with hir that most deperte
and hald thee with thy soverane,
for I had lever want ane harte
nor haif the hairt that dois me pane.
Thairfoir go, with thy lufe remane
and lat me leif thus unmolest.
Se that thou cum nocht agane,
bot byd with hir thou luvvis best.

2

Sen scho that I haif servit lang
is to depairt so suddanly,
addres thee now, for thou sall gang
and beir thy lady cumpany.
Fra scho be gon, hairtles am I,
for quhy thou art with hir possest:
thairfoir, my hairt, go hence in hy
and byd with hir thou luvis best.

3

Thocht this belappit body heir
be bound to servitude and thrall,
my fathfull hairt is fre inteir
and mind to serf my lady at all.

---

lever, rather. *byd*, remain. *hy*, haste. *at all*, in all respects.

Wald God that I wer perigall
under that redolent ros to rest!
Yit at the leist, my hairt, thou sall
abyd with hir thou lufis best.

4

Sen in your garth the lilly quhyte
may nocht remane amang the laif,
adew! the flour of haill delyte,
adew! the succour that ma me saif,
adew! the fragrant balme suaif
and lamp of ladeis lustiest.
My faithfull hairt scho sall it haif
to byd with hir it luvis best.

5

Deploir, ye ladeis cleir of hew,
hir absence, sen scho most deperte,
and specialy ye luvaris trew
that woundit bene with luvis darte,
for sum of you sall want ane harte
alsweill as I. Thairfoir at last
do go with myn with mind inwart
and byd with hir thou luvis best.

---

perigall, paregal, fully equal.

Bannatyne CCXC, ff.235a–b.

XL

1

RETURNE thee, hairt, hamewart agane
and byd quhair thou was wont to be.
Thou art ane fule to suffer pane
for luve of hir that luvis not thee.
My hairt, lat be sic fantesie.
Luve nane bot as they mak thee caus
and lat hir seik ane hairt for thee,
for feind a crum of thee scho fawis.

2

To quhat effect sowld thou be thrall
but thank, sen thou hes thy fre will?
My hairt, be not sa bestiall,
bot knaw quho dois thee guid or ill.
Remane with me and tary still
and se quha playis best thair pawis
and lat fillok ga fling hir fill.
for feind a crum of thee scho fawis.

3

Thocht scho be fair I will not fenyie,
scho is the kind of uthiris ma,
for quhy thair is a fellone menyie
that semis gud and ar not sa.

---

byd, remain. *feind a crum*, never a crumb.
fawis, cares. *pawis*, part. *fillok*, a giddy girl. *fenyie*, feign.
a fellone menyie, a miserable crew.

My hairt, tak nowdir pane nor wa
for Meg, for Merjory or yit Mawis,
bot be thou glaid and latt hir ga,
for feind a crum of thee scho fawis.

4

Becaus I find scho tuik in ill
at hir deperting, thou mak na cair,
bot all begyld go quhair scho will—
Beschrew the hairt that mane makis mair.
My hert, be mirry lait and air:
this is the fynall end and claus
and latt hir fallow ane filly fair,
for feind a crum of thee scho fawis.

_____

tuik in ill, took offence (at).
hir depairting, i.e. the preceding poem.

Bannatyne CCCXXVI, ff.252b–253a.

2.8 and 3.8. a crum, MS *accrum*. 4.4. Beschrew, MS
schrew.

100

SCOTT

XLI

1

How suld my febill body fure
the double dolour I indure?
The mornyng and the grit mallure
        can nane devyne
quhilk garris my bailfull breist conbure
to se ane uther haif the cure
        that suld be mine.

2

For weill I wait wes nevir wicht
wald sa infors his mind and mycht
to lufe and serf his lady bricht
        and want hir syne
as dois me martir day and nycht
without the only thing of rycht
        that suld be mine.

3

War I of pissans for to prufe
my lawty and my hairtly lufe,
I suld hir mind to mercy mufe
        with sic propyne:
war all the warld at my behufe,
scho suld it haif, be God abufe,
        that suld be mine.

---

fure, bear. *mallure*, misfortune. *conbure*, burn. *pissans*, puissance.
lawty, loyalty. *propyne*, gift.

4

Now quhome to sall I mak my mone,
sen trewth and constans find I none,
for all the fathfull lufe is gone
      of femenene.
It wald upros ane hart of stone
to se me lost for lufe of one
        that suld be mine.

5

Quha suld my dullit spreitis rais,
sen for no lufe my lady gais,
bot, and gud service mycht hir mais,
      scho suld incline.
I dre the dollour and diseis
quhen utheris hes hir as thay pleis
        that suld be mine.

6

I may persaif that weill be this,
that all the blythnes, joy and blis,
the lusty wantoun life, I wis,
      of lufe is hyne
and no remeid, sen so it is,
bot paciens, suppois I mis
        that suld be mine.

---

femenene, womankind. *upros*, uprouse. *mais*, sooth, soften.
hyne, hence, i.e., gone.

7

For nobillis hes nocht ay renown
nor gentillis ay the gayest gown.
Thay cary victuallis to the town
     that werst dois dine.
Sa bissely to busk I boun.
Ane uthir eitis the berry down
     that suld be myn.

8

Quha wald the rege of yowtheid dant,
lat thame the court of luvaris hant
and than as Venus subject grant
     and keip hir tryme.
Perchance thay sall find freindschip skant
and abill thair rewaird to want,
     as I did mine.

---

busk, bush. *boun*, hasten, speed. *tryme*, gracious.

Bannatyne CCCVI, f.244b.

2.5. as dois me, *and dois me* in MS, corrected to
as I do.

103

XLII

1

TO LUVE unluvit it is ane pane,
for scho that is my soverane,
sum wantoun man so he hes set hir
that I can get no lufe agane
bot brekis my hairt and nocht the bettir.

2

Quhen that I went with that sweit may
to dance, to sing, to sport and pley,
and oft times in my armis plet hir,
I do now murne both nycht and day
and brekis my hart and nocht the bettir.

3

Quhair I wes wont to se hir go
rycht trimly passand to and fro,
with cumly smylis quhen that I met hir—
and now I leif in pane and wo
and brekis my hairt and nocht the bettir.

4

Quhattane ane glaikit fule am I
to slay my self with malancoly,
sen weill I ken I may nocht get hir,
or quhat suld be the caus and quhy
to brek my hairt and nocht the bettir.

---

plet, entwined. *glaikit*, silly.

5

My hairt, sen thou may nocht hir pleis,
adew!—as gud lufe cumis as gais.
Go chus ane udir and foryet hir.
God gif him dolour and diseis
that brekis thair hairt and nocht the bettir.

Bannatyne CCCXXXIV, f.256a−b.

105

XLIII

1

IN JUNE the jem of joy and geme,
this present to compile expres,
but hurt, but wem, or wind to stem,
inarmit I am with havines,
wantone in weill but wo,
glaid without grief also
and fre of every fo
        that I confes.

2

I maik it plane for luve agane
thair sall no sorrow in me sink,
nor yit in vane to suffer pane
to stop frome sleip, frome meit or drink.
Thair is no lady fre
that, and scho favour me,
scho will nocht thoill to se
        me pine, I think.

3

Be scho content of cors and rent,
all salbe hirs that I may get hir:
will scho absent, hyne sall I went
and at als little valor set hir.

---

geme, sport. *present*, legal document. *wem*, scar.
cors and rent, body and income (legal phrase).
valor, value (legal term).

Quhair power ma not plais,
adew! without disais:
als gud luve cumis as gais,
      or rathir bettir.

4

Quhen scho growis heich, I draw on dreich
to vesy and behald the end:
quhen scho growis skeich, I byd on beich
to lat hir in the brydill bend:
quhen scho growis meik and tame,
scho salbe wylcome hame:
gif scho my luve quitclame,
      I sall not kend.

5

Pleis scho to rew, I sall persew
with subject service every sessone:
be scho untrew, fairweill! adew!
for as scho chaingis, I sall cheis one:
bot gif scho steidfast stand
and be not variand,
I am at hir command—
      conforme to ressone.

---

heich, haughty. *on dreich*, behind. *skeich*, skittish. *on beich*, aloof.
quit clame, disown, renounce (legal phrase).

Bannatyne CCCXXXII, f.255b.

107

XLIV

1

LEIF, Luve, and lat me leif allone
at libertie, subject to none,
for it may weill be sene upone
my bludles, blaiknit ble,
the tormenting in time bygon
that skers hes left bot skin and bon
throw fremmitnes of thee.

2

For thruch thy feid I find expres
my only lady merciles,
sa doggitly scho did me dres
with wo and misery:
quhen scho had welth and wantounes,
I had bot dollour and distres
throw fremmitnes of thee.

3

To confort hir thou wes inclynd
and hald my murning in my mind:
I fand hir of ane staffage kind,
bath staitly, strange and he.
Scho wes uncurtass and unkind:
it wes hir play to see me pynd
throw fremmitnes of thee.

---

blaiknit, pale. *ble,* complexion. *fremmitnes,* perverseness.
feid, feud. *doggitly,* cruelly. *staffage,* stubborn.

4

Thou held hir curage he on loft
and ted my tendir hairt lyk toft:
I knaw how costly I wes coft,
quhen scho yeid frank and fre:
thou sufferit hir to sleip full soft,
quhair mirthles I wes marterit oft
throw fremitnes of thee.

5

Cupeid, thou kennis I burd to knaw
the langsum leving in thy law,
bot this is nocht the first ourthraw
that thou hes done to me.
Bot of thee now I stand nocht aw,
sen Ressoun dois my benner blaw
aganis the feid of thee.

6

This lady is so gud ane gyd
scho lattis me nevir gang on syd
bot teichis me both time and tyd
recent befoir mine e,
quhome in to lippin and confyd
I slip and lattis all ourslyd
aganis the feid of thee.

---

ted, shook and scattered. *toft*, tow, hay. *coft*, bought.
burd, burned. *blaw*, i.e. unfurl. *on syd*, aside. *lippin*, trust.

Bannatyne CCCXIV, f.247a–b.

2.3. doggitly, MS *doggitles*. 4.4. frank and, MS *frankand*.

XLV

1

QUHA lykis to luve or that law pruve,
lat him beleif this life to leid:
his mind sall moif but rest or ruve
with divers dolouris to the deid:
he sall tyne appetyte
and meit and sleip gife quite
and want the way perfyte
  to find remeid.

2

He sall nocht wit quhiddir that it
be panefull, plesand, weill or wo
to stand or sit, remoif or flit,
to gang, to ly, to byd or go:
no wit salbe degest,
to heir, se, smell nor test,
bot as a brutall best
  he sall be so.

---

ruve, stop, stay. *wit*, sense (i.e., the five senses).
degest, composed, settled, fixed.

3

Fle thocht he wald, Lufe sall him hald
within the dungeoun of dispair,
quhyle hett, quhyle cald, a thousand fald
his purpois salbe heir and thair:
he sall hald wisdome vice
and vertew of no price
bot as a fule unwyce
        so sall he fair.

4

This is the quhy and caus that I
complene so peteously in plane:
I lufe the wy will nocht apply
nor grant to gife me grace agane:
the moir service I do,
the moir fremmit is scho
without respect unto
        my crewall pane.

5

Ye luvaris, se gife that this be
ane life that all gude men malingis.
I say for me it is to fle
aboif the pest and plaig that ringis,
quhilk is bot curius,
ay woid and furius
and fire sulfurius
        that men doun bringis.

---

wy, person. *apply*, be inclined. *fremmit*, perverse.
ringis, reigns. *curius*, full of care. *woid*, mad.

6

My brethir deir, we most forbeir
and fra this sinfull life evaid us.
Lat Ressoun steir your hairtis inteir
and nocht thoill lathly lust to leid us,
quhilk is the verry net
that Satane for us set
to caus us quyt foryet
      the Lord that maid us.

Bannatyne CCCLXXIV, ff.285b–286a.

112

XLVI

1

FRA RAIGE of youth the rink hes rune
and Ressone tane the man to tune:
the brukle body than is wune
and maid ane veschell new:
for than thruch grace he is begune
the well of wisdome for to kune:
than is his weid of vertew spune—
trest weill, this taill is trew.

2

For youth and will ar so consors,
without that wisdome mak devors,
thay rin lyk wild undantit hors
but brydillis to and fro:
thair curage sa ourcumis thair cors,
thrucht heit of blude it hes sic fors,
bot gif the mind haif sum remors
of God, all is ago.

---

tane . . . to tune, brought to a proper frame of mind,
tuned as an instrument. *wune*, i.e. saved.
kune, taste. *consors*, closely allied.

SCOTT

3

This wid fantastyk lust but lufe
dois so yung men to madnes mufe
that thay ma nowthir rest nor rufe
till thay mischeif thair sellis:
haif thay thair harlottis in behufe,
thay sussy nocht thair God abufe,
thair fame, thair wirschep, nor reprufe
off honour, nor ocht ellis.

4

Ferme luve with prudens suld be usit,
thocht sum allegeand to excusit
sayis that luve with witt inclusit
yit is nocht worth a buttoun.
Sic vane opinioun is confusit
that man but ressoun may be rusit:
quha bene with beistly lust abusit
I hald him bot ane muttoun.

5

Quha wald in luve be estimat
suld haif thair hairtis ay elevat
with merciall myndis in doing that
mycht caus thair fais to dowt thame:

---

wid, mad. *sellis*, selves. *behufe*, call, command, service. *sussy*, care about. *excusit*, excuse it, defend it (i.e. love and the habits of lovers). *inclusit*, shut in, controlled. *confusit*, i.e. foolish. *rusit*, extolled.

114

thocht wemen self be temerat,
thay luve no man effeminat
and haldis thame bot I wat not quhat
that can nocht be without thame.

6

Yit man suld favour thame, howbeid
thay be bot necessar of neid:
becaus we cum of thame in deid,
thair personis suld be prysit:
as grund is ordand to beir seid,
so is the woman born to breid
the fruct of man, and that to feid
as Nature hes devysit.

7

Schort to conclude, I wald bath knew
that luvaris suld be leill and trew
and ladeis suld all thingis eschew
that ma thair honor smot:
be permanent that wald persew
and rin nocht reklesly to rew
bot as I direct. Adew!
thus I depairt, quod Scott.

---

temerat, timid.

Bannatyne CCCLXVIII, f.280a–b.

4.3 sayis, MS *saying*. 5.8. nocht, MS *noth*.

XLVII

1

QUHEN I think on my lady deir,
war nocht Gud Hoip, I wald be schent:
sic panis to me thair can appeir
that I nocht wait quhair I sall went:
to bowne me than our busk and bent
it is non but for all my beir,
so am I vexit in mine entent
quhen I think on my lady deir.

2

Than is thair non to confort me
quhen I am standand in that stage:
suppois I wer in point till de,
thair is nocht wrey in wardlie wrege
to rug me than out of that rege.
Than cumis Gud Hoip with lachand cheir
and biddis me lat all sorrowis swage,
quhen I think on my lady deir.

---

schent, ruined. *bowne*, hasten, speed. *busk*, bush. *bent*, moor.
but, remedy. *beir*, outcry. *wrey*, *wrege*, (obscure). *rug*, pull.

3

'How sall I lat all sorowis ses,
Gud Hoip, I pray thee tell me this?
My lady may my cors incres
and all my hell turne untill blis.
I may be mad quhen I hir mis,
suppois I wald, this is no weir.
How may thou fra this warld me wis,
quhen I think on my lady deir?'

4

'Yit sall I wis thee fra this way,
sa thou tak heid unto my lair:
gif that thou luvis ane lady gay,
se thou be nevir in dispair:
suppois that scho be nevir so fair,
yit may thou fang hir to thy feir:
thairfoir be blyth bayth lait and air
quhen thou thinkis on thy lady deir.

5

Oft time hes bene hard and sene
ane loird hes luvit ane las full weill
and eik a laid ane lady scheyne:
so Luf of Fortoun turnis hir quheill:
suppois ane fremmit fair thou feill,
yit in hir service perseveir:
suppois that scho be stif as steill,
yit sall thou win thy lady deir.

---

ses, cease. *my cors incres*, i.e., give me new strength.
weir, doubtful point. *wis*, guide. *fang*, win. *feir*, mate.
fremmit, unhappy. *fair*, experience.

6

Gif thou luvis hir and scho nocht thee,
with wisdome yit thou may hir win,
thocht scho be cumd of grit degre
and thou be cumin of sempill kin:
so in hir service thou nocht blin
bot ay be curtas to that cleir,
and sa that gentrice be hir within,
sa sall thou win thy lady deir.'

7

Now to Gud Hoip I gif my hand
that I sall luf my lady best:
quhairevir I fair our se or land,
my hairt with hir sall evir moir rest:
syne do to me as evir scho lest,
for I am hiris quhill I am heir,
for in that fre my faith is fast
quhen I think on my lady deir.

---

blin, cease, desist. *gentrice*, gentle, noble behaviour.

Bannatyne CCXLIX, f.217a–b. See Introduction, pp. lxiii–lxv

3.5. may, MS *my*. 4.4. se, MS *si*.

XLVIII

1

The well of vertew and flour of womanheid
and perfyt patrone unto patiens,
lady of lawty bayth in word and deid,
rycht sobir, sweit, full meik of eloquens,
bayth gud and fair—to your magnificens
I me commend, as I haif done befoir
my sempill hairt for now and evir moir.

2

For evir moir I sall you service mak:
syne of befoir in to my mind I maid—
sen first I knew your ladischip—but lak,
bewty, youth of womanheid ye had,
withouttin rest my hairt cowth nocht evad:
thus am I youris, and evir sensyne hes bene,
commandit be your gudly twa fair ene.

3

Your twa fair ene makis me oft syis to sing,
your twa fair ene makis me to syche also,
your twa fair ene makis me grit conforting,
your twa fair ene is wyte of all my wo,
your twa fair ene, may no man keip thame fro
withouttin rest that gettis a sycht of thame:
this of all vertew beir ye now the name.

---

patrone, pattern. *maid*, represented. *lak*, fault.
sensyne, since. *wyte*, cause, blame.

SEMPLE

4

Ye beir the name of gentilnes of blud,
ye beir the name that mony for you deis,
ye beir the name ye ar bayth fair and gud,
ye beir the name that faris than you seis,
ye beir the name fortoun and ye aggreis,
ye beir the name of landis of lenth and breid,
the well of vertew and flour of womanheid.

---

that faris than you seis, which continues after your death.

Bannatyne CCLII, f.218a–b. Notice the use of
concatenatio to link stanzas (cf. XI and XII).

1.2. perfyt patrone, MS *patrone*. 3.4. wyte, MS wy^t =
wycht. 3.7 beir, MS *were*.

120

ANONYMOUS

XLIX

BE GLAID al ye that luvaris bene,
for now hes May depaynt with grene
the hillis, valis and the medis
and flouris lustely upspreidis.
Awalk out of your sluggairdy
to heir the birdis melody
quhois suggourit nottis loud and cleir
is now ane parradice to heir.
Go, walk upoun sum rever fair,
go, tak the fresch and holsum air,
go, luke upoun the flurist fell,
go, feill the herbis plesand smell
quhilk will your comfort gar incres
and all avoid your havines.
The new cled purpour hevin aspy:
behald the lark now in the sky:
with besy wing scho clymis on hicht
for grit joy of the dayis licht:
behald the verdour fresch of hew,
powdderit with grene, quhyt and blew,
quhairwith Dame Flora in this May
dois richely all the feild array,
and how Aurora with visage pale
inbalmes with hir cristall hale
the grene and tendir pylis ying
of every gres that dois upspring,
and with hir beriall droppis bricht
makis the gresys gleme of licht.

---

awalk, awake. *flurist*, flowery. *fell*, hill. *pylis*, blades.

ANONYMOUS

Luk on the saufir firmament
and on the annammellit orient.
Luke, or Phebus put up his heid,
as he dois rais his baneris reid,
he dois the eist so bricht attire
that all semis birnyng in a fire,
quhilk comfort dois to every thing,
man, bird, beist and flurissing.
Quhairfar, luvaris, be glaid and lycht,
for schort is your havy nycht
and lenthit is your myrry day.
Thairfoir ye welcum new this May.
And, birdis, do your haill plesance
with merry song and observance
this May to welcum at your mycht
at fresch Phebus' uprising bricht.
And, all ye flouris that dois spreid,
lay furth your levis upoun breid
and welcum May with benyng cheir,
the quene of every moneth cleir.
And every man thank in his mind
the God of Nature and of Kind
quhilk ordanit all for our behufe,
the erd undir, the air abufe,
bird, beist, flour, time, day and nycht,
the planeitis for to gif us licht.

---

flurissing, flowers. *upoun breid*, in full display.

Bannatyne CCLXXXI, f.229b.

L

MY HAIRT is heich aboif, my body is full of blis,
for I am sett in lufe als weill as I wald wis.
I lufe my lady pure and scho luvis me agane,
I am hir serviture, scho is my soverane,
scho is my verry harte, I am hir howp and heill,
scho is my joy inwart, I am hir luvar leill,
I am hir bound and thrall, scho is at my
    command,
I am perpetuall hir man both fute and hand.
The thing that may hir pleis, my body sall fulfill;
quhat evir hir diseis, it dois my body ill.
My bird, my bony ane, my tendir bab venust,
my lufe, my life allane, my liking and my lust,
we interchange our hairtis in utheris armis soft,
spreitles we twa depertis, usand our luvis oft:
we murne quhen licht day dawis, we plene the
    nycht is schort,
we curs the cok that crawis that hinderis
    our disport.
I glowffin up agast quhen I hir mys on nycht
and in my oxster fast I find the bowster richt.
Than langour on me lyis, lyk Morpheus,
    the mair,
quhilk causis me uprys and to my sweit repair,
and than is all the sorrow furth of remembrance
that evir I had a forrow in luvis observance.

---

heill, source of wellbeing, salvation. *venust*, charming.
dawis, dawns. *glowffin*, glare. *oxster*, arm. *bowster*, bolster.
furth of, gone from. *a forrow*, before.

ANONYMOUS

Thus nevir I do rest, so lusty a life I leid
quhen that I list to test the well of womanheid.
Luvaris in pane, I pray God send you sic remeid
as I haif nycht and day, you to defend frome deid.
Thairfoir be evir trew unto your ladeis fre
and thay will on you rew, as mine hes done
    one me.

Bannatyne CCLXXXV, f.231a–b.

LI

IN TO the nycht quhen to ilk wicht Natur
    derekis rest,
I walk allone, makand my mone, with
    luvis pane opprest.
Was nevir man sen luve began that
    luvit moir trewly
then I, I wis, suppois I mis the lufe of my lady.
In luvis dance sic is my chance to lufe
    unlovit agane:
heirfoir, allace! my cairfull cace, quhome to
    sall I complane?
Sall I me mene to Venus quene or to
    hir sone Cupyde
that with his dart thirlis my harte with
    wondis warkand wide?
Or for support sall I exort Mars god armipotent
to saif my life in to this strife, or sorrow
    do me schent?
For thocht I cry on my lady my dolour to redres,
for all my trewth scho hes no rewth on
    my daly distres.
It is hir joy to wirk me noy, hir weill to
    wirk me wo,
it is hir will that I lyk ill—allais! quhy
    dois scho so?

---

derekis, directs. *walk*. wake. *thirlis*, pierces. *schent*, ruin.
noy, harm.

125

It is hir cure to do plesure to him feling no pane
and latt me go, lamenting so with sichis
    and sorrowis slane.
More mirreit war to hir be far to cure the
    seik from cair
than to propine him medecyne that nevir
    felt no sair.
Bot mony man wise sayis that the gyse of luve
    is evir sway,
to sla the trew, and on him rew that falsast
    is of fay.
O nymphis thre, haif mind on me and cut
    my fatell threid,
sen in this erd ye gaif me werd nevir in
    lufe to speid.

---

cure, office. function. *mirreit*, merit. *propine*, prescribe.
sway, so. *werd*, fate, fortune.

Bannatyne CCCXVIII, f.249a.

LII

1

SO PRAYIS me as ye think caus quhy
and lufe me as you lykis best:
as pleisis you, so plesit am I:
gif nocht I find, of nocht I traist.

2

Gif ye be trew, I wilbe just:
gif ye be fals, flattery is fre
all times and houris, evin as ye lust,
for me till use als weill as ye.

3

Gif ye do mok, I will bot play:
gif ye do lawch, I will nocht weip:
evin as ye list think, do or say,
sic law ye mak, sic law I keip.

4

Schaw fathfull lufe, luve sall ye haif:
schaw dowbilnes, I sal you quyt:
ye can nocht use nor no ways craif
bot evin that same is my delyt.

---

lust, wish.

5

Bot gif ye wald be trew and plane,
ye wald me pleis and best content
and gif ye will nocht so remane,
as I haif said, so am I lent.

6

Avys you as ye think to do
and use me as ye list to find.
Quhat neidis lang talking thairto?
for as I am, ye knaw my mind.

7

Be war thairfoir and tak gud heid
quhat is the sentens of this bill,
for and ye beir me ocht at feid,
I sall you hald ay at ill will.

8

Thairfoir be trew but vairians
and I salbe as of befoir:
uthirwayis generis discrepans.
Content you—this ye get no moir.

---

lent, set. *sentens*, meaning. *bill*, letter, document, poem.
feid, feud, enmity.

Bannatyne CCCXXI, f.250a.

7.1. Be war, MS *Bewar*. 7.4. will, MS w.

LIII

1

O LUSTY flour of youth benyng and sweit,
fresch blome of bewty, blythfull,
   brycht and schene,
fair lufsum lady gentill and discret,
yung brekand blosum yit on the stalkis grene,
delytsum lilly lusty for to be sene,
be glaid in hairt and expell havines:
bair of blis that evir so blyth hes bene,
devoid langour and leif in lustines.

2

Brycht sterne at morrow that dois the
   nycht hyn chace,
of luvis lychtsum life the lamp and gyd,
lat no dirk clud absent fro us thy face
nor lat no sable frome us thy bewty hyd
that hes no confort quhair that we go or ryd
bot to behald the beme of thy brychtnes:
baneis all baill and into blis abyd:
devoid langour and leif in lustines.

---

devoid, cast aside. *sterne*, star.

3

Art thou nocht plesand lusty yoing and fair,
full of all vertew and gud conditioun,
rycht nobill of blud, rycht wyis and debonair,
honorable, gentill and faithfull of renoun,
liberall, lufsum and lusty of persoun?
Quhy suld thou than lat sadnes thee oppres?
In hairt be blyth and lay all dolour down,
devoid langour and leif in lustines.

4

I me commend with all humilitie
unto thy bewty blisfull and bening,
to quhome I am and sall ay servand be
with steidfast hairt and faithfull trew mening
unto the deid withoutyn deperting,
for quhais saik I sall my pen addres
sangis to mak for thy reconforting,
that thou may lief in joy and lustines.

5

O fair sweit blossum now in bewty flouris,
unfaidit bayth of cullour and vertew,
thy nobill lord that deid hes done devoir
faid nocht with weping thy vissage fair of hew.
O lufsum lusty lady wise and trew,
cast out all cair and comfort do incres,
exyll all sichand, on thy servand rew,
devoid langour and leif in lustines.

Bannatyne CCXCVIII, f.238b. David Laing in his edition
of Dunbar (2 vols., Edinburgh 1834: Supplement, 1865)

suggests that this poem was addressed to Queen
Margaret after the death of James IV at Flodden. It is
perhaps more likely that it was addressed to Queen
Mary on her return to Scotland after the death of her
husband, Francis II, in December 1560. Mary landed at
Leith on 19 August 1561. She was eighteen years old.

1.1. sweit, MS *bricht*, perhaps accidentally copied from
line 2.
2.2. the lamp, MS omits; *correxit* Schipper. 3.1. nocht,
MS omits.
4.5. withoutyn, MS *without*. 5.6. out all cair, MS *out all
out all cair.*

LIV

1

GIFE langour makis men licht
or dolour thame decoir,
in erth thair is no wicht
may me compair in gloir:
gif cairfull thochtis restoir
my havy hairt frome sorrow,
I am for evirmoir
in joy both evin and morrow.

2

Gif plesour be to pance,
I plaint me nocht opprest,
or absence micht avance,
my hairt is haill possest:
gif want of quiet rest
frome cairis micht me convoy,
my mind is nocht mollest
bot evirmoir in joy.

3

Thocht that I pance in pane
in passing to and fro,
I laubor all in vane,
for so hes mony mo

---

decoir, invest with honour. *pance*, think painful thoughts.
mollest, troubled.

that hes nocht servit so
in suting of thair sweit—
the nar the fire I go,
the grittar is my heit.

4

The turtour for hir maik
mair dule may nocht indure
nor I do for hir saik,
evin hir, quha hes in cure
my hart, quhilk salbe sure
in service to the deid
unto that lady pure,
the well of womanheid

5

Schaw, schedull, to that sweit
my pairt so permanent
that no mirth quhill we meit
sall caus me be content,
bot still my hairt lament
in sorrowfull siching soir
till time scho be present.
Fairweill. I say no moir.

---

suting, courting. *nar*, nearer. *turtour*, turtle-dove.
dule, sorrow. *schedull*, letter, poem. *pairt*, role.

Bannatyne CCCV, f.244a. The poem is presumably
addressed to Queen Mary before her marriage to
Darnley on 29 July 1565.

1.5. thochtis, MS *thoftis*. 4.6. in, MS *and*.

133

LV

1

Now in this mirthfull time of May
my dullit spreit for to rejos
I sall with sobir mind assay
gif I can ocht in metir glos—
syn all the poyntis of my purpois
in secreit wyis salbe asselyeit—
how in my garth thair growis a rois
wes fresche and fair and now is felyeit.

2

All winttir throcht this ros wes reid
and now in May it changis hew:
thairfoir I trow that it be deid
and als the stak that it on grew.
Suld I for plesour plant a new?
Na!—that I vow to God in plane:
said it fair weill, all flouris adew!
bot gif that rois revert agane.

---

glos, cover up, disguise. *asselyeit*, attacked.
felyeit, failed, withered. *revert*, return.

3

For of all plesans to my sycht
that grew on grund it beris the gre:
my hairt wes on that day and nycht,
it wes so plesand for to se.
Now thair is nowdir erb nor tre
sall grow within my garding mair
quhill I get wit quhat gart it de,
this foirsaid flour that wes so fair.

---

beris the gre, wins the victory.

Bannatyne CCLXII, f.222b. The poet obviously expects
his verses to be taken at something more than face value.
The rose may be Queen Mary after the murder of
Darnley in February 1567: Darnley, in turn, may be
'the stak that it on grew'. 'And now in May it changis
hew' may refer to the marriage of Mary and Bothwell
on 15 May 1567.

LVI

1

IRKIT I am with langsum luvis lair,
oursett with inwart siching sair,
for in the presone of dispair
  I ly,
seing ilk wicht gettis sum weilfair
  bot I.

2

My hairt is pynd and persit so with panis,
quhill teiris over my visage ranis
and makis the blud within my vanis
  to dry.
Quha ma sic greif resist aganis
  bot I?

3

My mad misfortoun dois me so commuve
that I may nowthir rest nor ruve
bot wary all the goddis abuve
  the sky
that every leid obtenis thair luve
  bot I

---

wary, curse. *leid*, person.

4

All nobill hairtis of nateur ar inclynd,
quhair thay find constance, to be kind:
thairfoir to me scho sowld hir mind
    apply,
sen non is for hir persone pynd
    bot I.

5

The facultie of famenene is so,
unto thair freind to be his fo,
syne menis him quhen he is ago
    for thy:
uncourtesly thus keill thay mo
    than I.

6

Thay covet not the man that thay may get
for him thay hald as propper det:
on strangeris ay thair myndis ar set
    to spy.
Thus mo bene fetterit with thair net
    nor I.

7

Grit fule I am to follow the delyte
of thame that hes no faith perfyte:

---

famenene, womankind. *menis*, lament. *for thy*, as a consequence.

thairfoir sic cumpany I quyt
     denny:
off all my wo hes non the wyt
     bot I.

8

Quhat woundir is thocht I do weip and pleid
this fellon crewall life I leid
the quhilk but dowt wilbe my deid
     in hy,
for every man obtenis remeid
     but I.

9

My lady hes ane hairt of stone so hard
on me to rew scho hes no regard,
but bustously I am debard
     ay by
and every man gettis sum reward
     bot I.

---

wyt, blame. *fellon*, miserably. *in hy*, quickly, at once.
bustously, roughly, rudely. *by*, aside.

Bannatyne CCCXXIX, f.253a–b.

1.1. langsum, MS *langum*. 3.2. that, MS *thy*.

LVII

1

Lyik as the dum solsequium with cair overcum
dois sorrow quhen the sone gois out of sicht,
hingis doun his heid and drowpis as deid,
    nor will not spreid
bot lowkis his levis throw langour all the nicht,
till fuliche Phetone ryis with quhip in hand
to purge the cristall skyis and licht the land.
Birdis in thair boure watis on that oure
and to thair king ane glaid gudmorrow geivis:
fra than that floure list not till loure
bot lawchis on Phebus, lowsing out his leivis.

2

Swa standis with me except I be quhair I may se
my lamp of licht, my lady and my luve:
fra scho depertis ane thousand dairtis
    in sindry airtis
thirlis thruch my havy hart but rest or ruve.
My countenance declairis my inward greif
and howp almaist dispairis to find releiff.
I dee, I dwyne: play dois me pine:
I loth on every thing I luik, allace!
till Titan mine upoun me schyne
that I reveiff thruch favour of hir face.

---

solsequium, sunflower. *lowkis*, locks up. *levis*, petals.
lowsing, loosing. *airtis*, directions. *thirlis*, pierce.
ruve, repose. *dwyne*, fade away. *Titan*, the sun.

3

Fra scho appeir in to hir spheir, beginnis to cleir
the dawing of my lang desyrit day:
than curage cryis on howp to ryis
   quhen he aspyis
the noysum nicht of absens went away.
No noyis fra I awalk can me impesche,
bot on my staitly stalk I flurich fresche:
I spring, I sprout, my leivis lyis out,
my cullour changis in ane hairtsum hew:
no moir I lowt bot standis up stout,
as glaid of hir for quhome I only grew.

4

O happy day, go not away! Appollo stay
thy chair frome going doun unto the west!
Off me thou mak thy zodiak that I may tak
my plesour to behald quhome I luve best!
Thy presens me restoris to life frome deth:
thy absens lykwayis schoris to cutt my breth.
I wis in vane thee to remane
sen *Primum Mobile* sayis me alwayis nay:
at least thy wane bring sone agane.
Fairweill with patience perfors till day.

---

dawing, dawning. *noyis*, misfortunes. *awalk*, awake.
impesche, hinder. *chair*, chariot. *Primum Mobile*, the
outmost celestial sphere which controlled the
movement of the others beneath it.

Bannatyne Duplicate MS 44, pp. 52–3.

140

LOVE LYRICS IN
SCOTTISH GAELIC

*

LVIII

1

Is MAIRG dá ngalar an grádh,
gé bé fáth fá n-abrainn é;
deacair sgarachtainn ré pháirt;
truagh an cás i bhfeilim féin.

An grádh-soin tugas gan fhios,
ó's é mo leas gan a luadh,
mara bhfaigh mé furtacht tráth,
biaidh mo bhláth go tana truagh.

An fear-soin dá dtugas grádh,
's nach feadtar a rádh ós n-aird,
dá gcuireadh sé mise i bpéin,
gomadh dó féin bhus céad mairg.

2

Atá fleasgach ar mo thí,
a Rí na ríogh go rí leis!
a bheith sínte ré mo bhroinn
agus a choim ré mo chneis!

1

ALAS for him whose sickness is love,
for what cause soever I should say it;
hard it is to be free of it;
sad is the plight in which I am myself.

That love which I have given in secret,
since it profits me to declare it not,
if I find not quick relief,
my bloom will be slight and meagre.

He to whom I have given love,
since I cannot speak it openly,
if me he should put in pain,
may himself have cause to say a
    hundred times, alas!

2

There is a youth intent upon me,
King of kings, may he come to fortune!
Would that he were stretched by my body,
his breast to my breast!

NÍ MHEIC CAILÉIN

Dá mbeith gach ní mar mo mhian,
ní bhiadh cian eadrainn go bráth,
gé beag sin dá chur i gcéill,
's nach tuigeann sé féin mar tá.

Acht ní éadtrom gan a luing,
sgéal as truaighe linn 'nar ndís;
esan soir is mise siar,
mar nach dtig ar riar a rís.

W.J.Watson *Scottish Verse from the Book of the Dean of Lismore* (Scottish Gaelic Texts Society, Edinburgh 1937), pp. 234–5 and 307–8.

NÍ MHEIC CAILÉIN

Were all according to my desire
there would ne'er be distance between us,
though that be all too little to say,
seeing that he himself understands not
    how things are.

But it is not easy unless his ship come,
a tale that is most grievous to us both;
he is east and I am west,
so that our mutual desire comes not
    to pass again.